I AM A CROSS-POLLINATOR

Afrikologist Thought Experiments for Leaders Navigating from Ego-Ism to Eco-Ism

Musa Nxumalo

COPYRIGHT

I AM A CROSS-POLLINATOR

By Musa Nxumalo

Published in South Africa in 2020 by Knowledge Connections (Pty) Ltd, Pretoria, Gauteng.

First Edition

Print ISBN 978-1-990937-35-4

eBook ISBN 978-1-990937-36-1

Audio Book ISBN 978-1-990937-37-8

Edited by Michael W. Solomon
Illustrations & Graphics by Victor Chauke, AVAV Media

Layout, eBook conversion and online bookstore distribution by
www.bulabuka.co.za

Printed and bound by Novus Print, Montague Gardens, Paarl – a division of Novus Holdings

CONTENTS

DEDICATION

To *ugogo u*M.O, my paternal grandmother. uMaNsibande, okaMangcama, for being my light

To my children, Zama-Zwide and Nkosinathi Nxumalo, who are bravely diving deep into a life that is changing at an alarmingly rapid pace.

To them, and all other children of the world, I say:

"The future belongs to those who believe in the beauty of their dreams."

ACKNOWLEDGEMENTS

I would like to express my sincere gratitude to:

My fellow co-founder of Knowledge Connections, Vezi Mncwango, who has become the big brother I never had. *"Mpangazitha, kwande nje (abundance always)."*

Our administrator and project coordinator, Mosidi Mabe, for working tirelessly behind the scenes and for making our work at Knowledge Connections a walk in the park.

My coach, David Brown, for sacrificing his Monday mornings, to meet with me at 07h30 at Grey Owl, Centurion, without fail for the entire book development process.

Michael W. Solomon, the editor, for his immense contribution to the quality of this work, his guidance and for allowing us to tap into his well of wisdom; and, for always making himself available to do more than I ask for.

All our team members, for taking this work to every corner of South Africa, every nook and cranny of Africa and all major centres around the world.

Everyone who participated directly and indirectly in the interviews, the research stage, and in the validation and proof of concept engagements.

All that we have achieved as a team, and fellow cross-pollinators, is because you carried me on your backs when I couldn't walk on my own, and you allowed me to stand on your shoulders to see beyond what my body frame enables me to see.

"Thank you Musa for your invitation to connect to the oneness of all people as we step into our roles as Cross-Pollinators. This beautiful book teaches insightful life and leadership principles while taking us on a beautiful journey of the love story between Motho Fela and Kholofelo. As they face trials and tribulations in post-apartheid South Africa, Musa Nxumalo provides opportunities for readers to look within and access their authentic self, the value of the pause, patience and perseverance, the duality of inwardness and outwardness, transforming pain into positive energy amongst many more gems that can enable you to create a meaningful life of freedom and contribution."

NICOLE SORRELL

Partner, Lumina Learning, Camberley (Surrey, UK)

"In my interaction with the author himself, both prior and post writing of the book, I have experienced an invitation by him to share a personal journey of translating everyday life experiences into lessons about how to traverse treacherous terrains, avert risks and seize opportunities to achieve growth, sustainability and ultimately a shared prosperous future.

I think the book has a promise to reveal truths about life, which we often take for granted, mainly drawn from a careful observation of nature's own processes, here depicted, e.g. through the life of an insect, the bee which both leaders and ordinary folk alike will find, I believe, valuable lessons from."

TM MASUTHA (ADV.)

Former Minister of Justice and Correctional Services

"I believe this to be, one of the most profound observations on the challenges we face in this country, how we got here, and how each of us can take responsibility through cross-pollination, in our own society.

Musa Nxumalo, looks at South African society and cross–racial relationships through the eyes of his central character Motho Fela, a white Afrikaans mining engineering graduate caught up in a multi-cultural South Africa, 20 years post democracy. The dilemmas that Motho Fela faces are those that we all come across, and sadly, all too often rationalise, ignore or hope that someone else will fix. Apart from being an absorbing read, 'I Am a Cross-Pollinator' is a heart-warming, encouraging and yet challenging story that suggests that our future, and those of our children and grand-children, lie more in our hands than those of our politicians and captains of industry.

For leaders running diverse organisations and communities as well as coaches and practitioners in the leadership and change space, this is a must read."

BERNARD KOCH

Leadership & Strategy Development Coach, Kagera Consulting (Pty) Ltd

"When all is said and done, re *batho fela* – we are just human. 'I am a Cross-Pollinator' takes you on a human journey that will lead you back to self, back to who you really are, *Motho Fela*. That is a journey that will allow you to see *batho fela* (just people /fellow human beings) in everyone around you and appreciate the positive impact cross- pollination can make in society, business and at individual level"

KULANI SHILUVANE

Founder and Chief Consultant at Shiluvah HR and Labour Law Consultancy

"This book could not have come at a more opportune time to address a pressing need in our existence on planet earth. As humanity we need to be reminded of who we are and our connectedness to one another even though we may be divided by distance, belief systems, cultures, worldviews, gender and skin pigmentation, etc. The bottom line is, we come from one source. Musa, through his storytelling and core message is calling us to remember and to be anchored on what matters most - our collective humanity - and his call comes at an important juncture in the history of humankind and our habitat - planet earth. The message is clear - we are co-joint and we better wake up to that reality. We cannot succumb to big egos to destroy what is left of our essence and of Mother Earth. This book calls on leaders and all of us to stand and pull ourselves out of this dark quagmire of egoism. We ignore Musa's clarion call to our own peril"

Dr JERRY GULE

Chief Executive Officer, Institute of Personnel Management

FOREWORD

Fasten your seat belts. Settle in for a ride. Be prepared for pit stops where you'll be invited to answer questions designed to loosen up and surface your deepest thoughts.

I Am A Cross-Pollinator: Afrikologist Thought Experiments for Leaders Navigating from Ego-ism to Eco-ism - the book title is a mouthful, but is true to Musa Nxumalo's intent.

Musa offers you a uniquely South African love story that has a global trajectory. It traverses the personal, the professional, and the political terrain. Geographically, the protagonists Motho Fela (Gert du Toit) and Kholofelo (Sekwati) are strongly rooted in the mining towns of the Witwatersrand and villages of Limpopo. As their relationship and professional lives evolve over decades so expands their world view and their inter-continental, intellectual and activist engagement in global issues, especially on land; the geo-politics around the question of water and the environment. Motho Fela, over the years, becomes the cross-pollinating Afrikologist, modelling the leadership approach that Nxumalo advocates in his capacity as a coach.

You won't agree with everything in the book. I can hear the background murmur of people who are sceptical about *ubuntu* as it pertains to gender equality. And some would have preferred Kholofelo to be the leading figure rather than the supporting act who becomes Mev du Toit. She's the one at the beginning of the story who introduces Motho Fela to the poetry of Maya Angelou and is at that time the more politically aware of the couple.

But there is a saying that is powerful, "Not everything needs to be perfect, in order for it to be perfect." And in that spirit this is a courageously perfect book. Musa Nxumalo has poured his heart, soul and personal intellectual journey into these pages and generously offers his readers a fable that covers a broad span of topics that will provoke you to reflect on:

Identity: Who are you? Where are you coming from? Who are the ancestors that shaped you and walk with you into your future as part of your unseen entourage?

Race: Motho Fela's unlearning and new learning, as he first makes judgements of black culture using his white frame of reference and then reconsiders his mistaken assessments. Kholofelo is irritated by the non-compliments she receives that use skin colour descriptors that are food related – coffee, caramel, honey, chocolate. There's a consistent weave into the story of deep issues sometimes lightly told. One of the strengths of Musa's book is that it is never heavy, preachy or judgmental – the storyline is always there to make you think whilst maintaining the pace of the narrative.

Gender. You will eventually meet overt feminist, Nandi Sibiya, who speaks her truth and puts her fellow delegates on the line. Nandi has the wonderful quality of being strong whilst maintaining her warmth. Musa here once again skilfully weaves in some of his personal leadership lessons.

Corruption: From the descriptions of continuing poverty of mining communities to navigating through tender procedures and observation of malpractice – Musa Nxumalo is unsparing in revealing to readers the sorry-side of South Africa. One moment he describes the ostentatious branded accessories that seem to be part of the outfit of being involved in tenderpreneurship. And then he offers poignancy- when tenderpreneurs are called to account: what does this mean at a very personal domestic level? We witness the pain of a young boy, the friend of Motho Fela's son who's psychologically scarred having witnessed his father's arrest on charges of corruption.

Leadership Strategy- The young Motho Fela is instrumental in approaching conflict resolution through inclusivity and collaboration. This is a golden thread throughout the 20-year-time line, culminating in the story of an international education programme for environmental activists and public servants.

Musa Nxumalo has taken stock of the state of the world, the world in which he is an actor, the world that will be inherited by his children and grandchildren. I have a sense of Nxumalo pulling together his life's experience to date. It is rich and varied. He references the ten most critical problems of the world according to millennials. In "I am a Cross Pollinator" Musa harnesses his gift and heritage of story-telling. He accesses all his acquired skills as a leadership coach. He chooses the uncomfortable role of an activist, drawing inspiration from the words of Edmund Burke, "The only thing necessary for the triumph of evil is for good men and women to sit and do nothing." Musa could not sit and do nothing. Instead he's chosen to sit and write. The outcome is this crafted 2020 thought-leadership offering that deserves to be read as a clarion call to action.

Dr HELENA DOLNY

Founder of Grey Matters; world acclaimed leadership coach; consultant & facilitator on Time to Think; author of "Before Forever After: When conversations about living meet conversations about dying."

PREFACE

I am Musa, the Coach

I AM a Cross-Pollinator. I wasn't aware of this all along. But, now that my eyes have been opened to this new identity, it is clear to me that I have been a Cross-Pollinator from a very young age. Being a Cross-Pollinator is an identity that defines my outlook on life, my mission on planet earth, the multiple roles I play and the beliefs that guide me as I do my work.

I am a teacher. I am a coach. I am a storyteller. In my teaching and coaching practice, I use storytelling. It is one of the most powerful tools I know. It is also a skill, which I inherited from my grandmother, M.O, who continues to be my spiritual guide to this day. I see myself as a conduit of information and knowledge, for equipping people with alternative thinking tools, so that they can create more abundance.

My name is **Musawenkosi**, which, when broken down, translates to u**Musa** (*Grace, Mercy, Kindness*) **we** (*of*) **nkosi** (*God, the Lord*). My parents gave me this name in gratitude to God, for giving me a second chance, on day one of my life. I was assumed to be a still-born child, because I never cried, to take my first breath, when I was born. Had it not been for the German Missionary, Sr Reinolda Mey OSB, uMashiyane's (*her Zulu nickname, the people of Nongoma's Benedictine Hospital had given her because of her rather thick eyebrows*) insistence to everyone who was present in that maternity ward, on prayer and meditation, I wouldn't have made it.

In February 2018, after I had just turned forty two, while I was on a flight layover in Bole, Ethiopia, connecting to Mumbai, India, I was delighted to learn that Musa is a common name in the Horn of Africa

But, it means something else. The first part **Mu** – means *pool,* and **sah** – means *to draw from.* It suggests that one is a pool of water that people can draw from. The name Moses and Musah, are one and the same thing. We use those names interchangeably. They mean the same thing.

I am told, my people originally come from where the River Nile begins. It is a place where Hapi, the god of the Nile, is said to dwell, at the foothills of the Mountains of the Moon. In that area are mountains like Rwenzori on the Ugandan side, and Kilimanjaro if you approach it from Kenya or Tanzania.

We settled in South Africa around 1100 AD, if linguistic evidence and oral folklore are anything to go by. My grandmother would never miss an opportunity to tell stories about the ancient history of our people, in the evenings, when the entire family gathered around crackling coal fires in her hut. I was fascinated by her stories. She had a profound impact on me as a child. She was a multi-talented woman, who had been a teacher in Swaziland (eSwatini), in her early years, but later devoted herself to helping women throughout Zululand, 'who could not bear children' and whose marriages were at the brink of failure. She would invite them over to our compound, and they would stay for three to six months with us (while visiting their homes now and again). She never charged them lodging or consultation fees. After their children were born, they would come back to her with their happy husbands, and give her goats, chickens, turkeys and cows as a token of their gratitude. And I would ask her, what she did to change their situation, and she would say, "it's not the rain water I make them drink every day at sunrise, it's the change in the conversations they have with themselves internally. The mind has amazing powers. My job is to help people switch their modes of thinking, to tap into that mind power. That's all."

My great-grandfather was said to be one of the first people who encountered the European missionaries, who introduced Christianity to Northern Zululand, in the late 1880s. When I was a young boy, it was quite common to have white people visiting our compound, in the village. Even though this was in the early 1980s, people still regarded it as progressive. In a way that explained how slow the process of racial integration had been in our neck of the woods.

When I moved on to high school, at Inkamana, in Vryheid, I experienced my first real cross-pollination process. One of my teachers, Sr Francis OSB, a German-American nun, linked us up with other teenagers in America and Germany through a pen-pal system. Writing letters to age mates on the other side of the Atlantic and the Mediterranean, beyond what my minds' eye could see, impacted me immensely.

This evolved from virtual experiences to real experiences when I entered the world of work, first as a 'vacation student' and later as a young engineer-in-training at Anglo-American's Vaal River Operations, in Orkney, in the North West Province.

Vaal Reefs was a melting pot of cultures, African; Asian; American and European, and this took my understanding of diversity to another level entirely.

It was only in 2017, when I went to study human-centred design; social innovation and leadership, at the Bangkok based DSIL Global Academy, that I began to integrate my experiences in mining, engineering, education and entrepreneurship into a framework for reimagining the duties of leaders. The following year, I went on to get training on psychometric testing and leadership coaching through Lumina Learning, a UK based organization.

Our coaching practice is all about cross-pollination, because that's what encapsulates our values, beliefs and aspirations as a firm.

Why I Wrote this Book

After reading an article by Tanza Loudenback and Abby Jackson, in Business Insider, titled "The 10 Most Critical Problems in the World, according to Millennials", which summarizes the results of the World Economic Forum's Global Shapers Survey, I was forced to change my mind about 18 to 35 year olds. Far from being apathetic, as some would have us believe, they are deeply concerned about global issues. I found myself saying "I don't want to be remembered as one of those people who failed our youth, and humanity in general, when I had a chance to make a meaningful contribution to change".

The issues that came out of the survey were:

- Lack of economic opportunity and unemployment
- Safety/security/well-being
- Lack of education
- Food and water security
- Government accountability, transparency/corruption
- Religious conflicts
- Poverty
- Inequality (Income Discrimination)
- Large scale conflict/wars
- Climate change/destruction of nature

This resonated with me very strongly. It matched what I had been mulling over for years; especially the question of inequality. South Africa is one of the most unequal societies in the world. I saw this growing up in Nongoma, in Northern KwaZulu-Natal and throughout my life journey, in all the places I have lived.

My work, as a coach, has given me insight into why inequality is not going anywhere anytime soon. There is no way I can sit and do nothing, given all the privileges I now enjoy and the access to information that I have.

One of the most painful observations I have made over the years, is the question of how, inequality, relates to a multitude of other issues. In the top five, on that list, is what I think of as the RAT race, referring to three common complaints that we hear in coaching conversations.

They don't pay me enough	**Rands**
I hate my boss	**Authority**
That place is so toxic	**Toxicity**

The questions around money, capital, reward, compensation, and salaries feature very prominently whenever people talk about their jobs. Following that is the issue of authority, power, roles, responsibility, accountability, decision-making and so on. All of that happens within a culture that people see as toxic, emotionally draining, peculiar, foreign, exceptionally un-African.

All this stirs me at the core of my being, when I do my work as a leadership & behavioural dynamics coach in organizations. My main conviction and motivation is summed up beautifully in the words of Edmund Burke:

"The only thing necessary for the triumph of evil is for good men and women to do nothing."

INTRODUCTION

The Paradigm: Afrikology

South Africa is considered to be the Cradle of Humankind. This is where it all began. This book is written from a paradigm that asserts and interprets this historical and archaeological discovery. The context and content material is packaged and delivered from the Afrikologist perspective. It is the shade within which all this work is positioned.

The Afrikologist approach to knowledge production and consumption is a duality – it is both a form of protest and a way of seeking solutions. It bravely asks questions such as "What is our uniquely African way of teaching, learning and knowing? How can we bring our classic pedagogies into contemporary and modern methods of holistic human development?"

Afrikology creates a safe space for knowledge producers, merchants and consumers, to interface scientific knowledge and other forms of knowledge with indigenous knowledge systems for the advancement of the human experience.

In the 2011 African Books Collective review, Dani W. Nebudere from Uganda says "...in this way, Afrikology responds to the crisis created by the fragmentation of knowledge through existing academic disciplines. It advances trans-disciplinarity and hermeneutics to a level where they attain a coherent basis for interacting with Afrikology as an epistemology which returns wholeness to understanding and knowledge production."

James Hoggan, in his book, *I'm Right and You're an Idiot*, in the second edition where he talks about "The Toxic State of Public Discourse and How to Clean it Up, says:

"The most pressing environmental problem we face today is not climate change. Rather it is pollution in the public square, where a smog of adversarial rhetoric, propaganda and polarization stifles discussion and debate, creating resistance to change and thwarting our ability to solve our collective problems."

The most progressive way for us to handle issues about our shared past, present and future, is to follow the honey bee example, which is an empowering cross-pollination process, using Afrikologist methodologies.

Cross-Pollination: The Dance of Bees from Anthers to Stigmas

The Afrikologist approach to leadership puts a strong emphasis on doing things collaboratively, in a communal and inclusive way. This approach puts the ego aside, and brings to the centre of the stage the ecosystem within which we have to work with each other.

As Africans, we are social in our approach to life. Exclusion, classism and elitist ways of doing things are foreign to us. We are one with nature. We derive our identity and sense of being from all human beings around us, the entire animal kingdom, the mountains and the rivers plus all the flora and fauna. Raising our status to a level above plants and animals is an arrogance, that we treat with disdain, in the true Afrikologist philosophy.

We use totems, and symbols, that are linked with nature, associating ourselves with particular animals and plants, to articulate not only our identity, but also our purpose and our reason for being. Our surnames, clan names, praise songs and poems are full of such details.

In Zulu classic art forms, the King's praise singer is called *iNyosi* (the Bee). In his prose, satire and song, he is charged with the duty of stinging while bringing honey and pollen. INyosi, therefore, is associated very strongly with leadership matters, as he plays a critical role in shaping leadership behaviour and drawing the nation's attention to what leadership is and how he thinks leadership should be.

The praise singer recognizes and acknowledges everyone to be a flower, and therefore, worthy of receiving pollen for them to be fruitful in their own lives. To a large degree, individual lives reflect the psyche at national leadership levels. Reciting these poems and praise songs, gives the praise singer, an opportunity to bridge the gap between ordinary folk and their leaders. That is a classic African way of carrying pollen between anthers and stigmas.

The transfer of pollen from the male reproductive organ in a flower, an anther or a male cone, of one plant to the female reproductive organ, a stigma or a female cone, of another plant, by the action of wind, insects and other animals, is called cross-pollination. This is a beautiful natural process that increases the genetic diversity of a plant population, by increasing the number of heterozygous individual plants. Mechanisms that promote cross-pollination include male flowers on one plant and female flowers on another, having pollen that is mature, before the stigmas on the same plant are chemically receptive to being pollinated, and having anatomical arrangements, such as stigmas that are taller than anthers, that make self-pollination less likely. So begins the process of germination of the fruit; the bearing of seeds; and the birth of a new plant that later repeats the process within that ecosystem.

The best leaders, operate exactly the same way as what happens in a cross-pollination process. They apply the same abundance mentality, which is similar to how nature operates. Their ego does not matter, but the ecosystem within which they are called to lead, is the most important factor of their pace, direction and style. The leader draws lessons from all of nature.

Plants are governed by an intelligence that gives them the innate abilities to know what to do when, in a well-orchestrated fashion, which to a casual observer will look like magic. It is not magic. It is the understanding of the laws of nature, and having the humility to learn them and practice them.

The process of cross-pollination happens in a culture receptive to new progressive ideas and opens up space for possibilities in line with organizational goals. In such a culture, people bring their best game, when they come to work.

Tom Kelley, when talking about cross-pollination, in his book *Ten Faces of Innovation*, says:

"The cross-pollinator draws associations and connections between seemingly unrelated ideas or concepts to break new ground. Armed with a wide set of interests, an avid curiosity, and an aptitude for learning and teaching, the cross-pollinator brings in big ideas from the outside world to enliven their organization. People in this role can often be identified by their open mindedness, diligent note-taking, tendency to think in metaphors, and ability to reap inspiration from constraints"

Leadership Navigation Tool: The #B3MB Decision Making Model

At the centre of all leadership challenges, is the ability for leaders to make quality decisions. All the problems and challenges that we face today, in the world, arise because the majority of our leaders are unable to navigate the narrow spaces of decision making. Accountability, integrity and clarity of mind are fast becoming rare leadership qualities. Our leaders are compromised on many levels, and that is why we end up unable to handle even the simplest of all the challenges facing us.

Leadership, and decision making in particular, is a lot like driving a car. Driving a car involves a lot of continuous observation. Decisions made while driving all have to do with what the driver is able to see, and process that information quickly, to make decisions about slowing down; accelerating; turning left; turning right; giving way to others; putting on the wipers; sounding the hooter or adjusting the mirrors to get a better view.

In South Africa, we have what we call K-53, which is a test used for driver's license assessments. In that test, there are five observation points they drill in to the minds of novice drivers – Blind Spot; Mirror; Mirror; Mirror; Blind Spot.

This book introduces that concept, as a tool for decision making, that leaders should consider the following when making decisions:

1. Blind Spot on the left (history/past/old data/old experiences/the journey up to that point)
2. Mirror on the left (vision/clarity/visual acuity/visual range/information available to them)
3. Mirrors in the middle (new past that is unfolding/dashboard/indicators and meters/now)
4. Mirror on the right (context/prevailing situation/others/passengers/the vehicle itself)
5. Blind Spot on the right (the future/limitations/capabilities/new information/skills to see).

SECTION 1: BLINDSPOT (THE PAST)

"The present is where we get lost - if we forget our past and have no vision of the future"

Ayi Kwei Armha

1. ALIENATION

The Essence of Being Human

Deep in the belly of the earth lies a huge web of human bones. In South Africa, this web is shaped like a soup bowl facing up, as if a beggar is holding it, from deep within. It stretches from Ekurhuleni, in the East Rand, where it is a bit shallower, all the way to Carletonville, on the border between Gauteng and North West provinces, where it is the deepest, and right across to the Free State, in Virginia and Welkom, where it is closer to the surface again. There are pockets elsewhere, in places like Barberton in Mpumalanga, and in Limpopo. This intricately woven human creation tells a painful story of how much we have eroded what the essence of being human, *ubuntu*, is all about. Each node, tells of ill-conceived ideas about what this land of plenty could potentially offer all those who live in it. Each thread, talks of how blind we have been to the gravely damaging effects of chasing this evasive, shiny commodity, called gold.

The boundary around this web, which ties it all together, seals the narrative off, highlighting how unskilful we have been, and still continue to be, in handling matters of the human experience at work. Thousands and thousands of lives have been lost, in mining and other related industries, over the last hundred and thirty years or so, since our insatiable pursuit of material wealth began. The work procedures, rules and regulations that we see today in our environmental and labour laws were not written in ink, they were written in blood. Human blood.

From as far back as the late 1880s, the gold and diamond mines sourced their labour from rural villages and the hinterlands of Southern Africa. Tribal chiefs and head men would offer their village young men to go and work for a penny or two per month, on annual conscription contracts in the cities of Johannesburg and Kimberly. Years later, in 1902, after the devastating effects of the

Anglo Boer War (the South African War) to the mining industry, The Employment Bureau of Africa, TEBA was established. Its main purpose was to support mines in meeting one of the country's key national priorities at the time, which was to expand mineral production. The mines were in dire straits. They had been mothballed by the war.

One such village, where unskilled labour was sourced, was Ga-Mohlala in Burgersfort. It is a typical sleepy yet serene Limpopo traditional settlement with clues and hints of an old-world we come from. It is dotted with hut sized boulders that protrude from the landscape like giant anthills. It is part of the tribal land of the BaPedi Marota Mamone kingdom. These spectacularly beautiful rock formations impacted the heart and mind of Kholofelo, a young girl who grew up in the royal household, seeing these amazing features of nature all around her. Every time when she went to school, she would ask herself what had brought those boulders there, and what was possibly inside of them. She would wonder what would come out if she found herself a giant knife and sliced them up. Perhaps a big snake would roll out, or lots of water would pour out. Lucky for her there was no chance of any serpentine undulation into her peaceful village, or surprise seepage of water from those rocks.

Her father was a tribal chief, who proudly traced his lineage all the way to Sekwati the first, the founding father of the BaPedi Marota nation. Her mother was an educator, sent to the area because of the scarcity of mathematics teachers at high school level, back in the early 1980s. Kholofelo loved school. She was one of those girls who defied all the prevailing circumstances that rural life imposed on local people. Her school was one of those typically South African rural village schools, where you will find seventy two children entombed in a classroom, very stuffy, with broken windows everywhere and limited desks and chairs. Yet, such schools, even today, still manage to produce high grades in mathematics; physics and chemistry. Despite those limiting conditions, she excelled in all her subjects. When she graduated from high school, she managed to get a bursary from the mines in Johannesburg to go learn about the rocks that she grew up surrounded with.

There were two strong women who influenced her as a young girl, and helped her to look beyond those limitations. They did visualization exercises with her, which were aimed at helping to see what else was out there in the world. It was her mother, who was a liberated city woman, who grew up in the townships in Pretoria. She exposed her to the culture of reading, as a desperate attempt to get her little girl to gain access to how life was beyond the confines of Ga-Mohlala. Then it was her teacher, Ma'am Mamabolo, who was one of those rare teachers who didn't believe that she held all knowledge, and because of her authority, she could suppress all other voices in her classroom. She encouraged her pupils to work together; have fun; learn from each other, through each other and with each other. Kholofelo kept the faith, as her name suggests, believing that deep within she was good enough; she was bigger than her circumstances and that she could achieve anything she put her mind to.

It came as no surprise to them, when Kholofelo said she wanted to study geology at Wits University, in 1994. As an 18 year old, she was clear about what she wanted to do with the rest of her life. She dedicated her first year on campus to translating what she had observed for years growing up in her village into practical application. In her mind she thought geology would help her solve the water scarcity issues in her village, and the country at large. She was excited about the opportunity presented to her by studying geology, which was a chance to learn about what she used to see every day back at home, on her way to fetch water from the local stream – the slow turning wheels on top of mining shaft head gear shining in the horizon, which to her, signalled that there was a lot going on deep in the belly of the earth.

Burgersfort is the land of platinum; palladium; uranium and chrome. It is rich in all respects, below the surface and above ground. The reef lines threaded between rock formations underground carry precious minerals of enviable quality. The fauna and flora, above all of that, is equally precious and a pleasure to the soul to the Pedi people. The mines in Burgersfort are not as old as the gold and diamond mines in the country.

Little did she know that life would throw her a sweet and refreshingly liberating opportunity for miscegenation, before the end of her first semester at Wits University. It changed her world and her life's trajectory completely. She met Motho Fela, a lanky Afrikaans fellow with dark curly hair, in the corridors at the Wits School of Mines building on West Campus. Boys were the last thing on her mind. But, being the shining light that she was, her personal magnetism was stronger and deeper than the shallow and petty race and identity forces at play in South Africa at the time. It was love at first sight.

Motho Fela, was not brought up in a village, and also, was not a city dweller either. He was born in Fochville, a tiny gold mining and agricultural town which is a stone's throw away from the world's deepest gold mine, Western Deep Levels, about a hundred kilometers west of Johannesburg. That's what the mine was called back in the 1980s when he grew up. He was already over twenty one when they met.

His mother was also a teacher, but she taught primary school. That commonality was what initially sparked a conversation between the two of them. Even though they had both been brought up by teachers, their material conditions were totally different from each other. The racial divide at work was not just along racial lines, but it was also on salary scales and pay grades. Motho Fela's mother was retired then. Her family emigrated from Liverpool, England, to South Africa because her father had been offered a lucrative job on the coal mines of Dundee, in KwaZulu-Natal. Motho Fela's father had been an inspector of mines almost all his life. He had worked his way up, from his humble beginnings as a learner official at Vaal Reefs all the way to being a high ranking official at the Department of Minerals and Energy Affairs.

When he retired, he and his wife chose to spend their lives quietly, away from all the politics and drama. They went into bee keeping. They loved bees, and they thought if they were to supply honey to all the curio shops in the West Rand and the Vaal, they would keep busy and fit, and never have to contend with old age health issues. Their plot of land was big enough, and the orchard that took up most of it, was now going to come into good use.

When Motho Fela finished high school, all his father wanted him to do was to follow in his footsteps, and go into mining. That's where the money was. So he thought. Being the obedient son, he joined Anglo-American's mines in Orkney, starting off as a learner official as well. Much to his father's delight, right after obtaining his N3 in mining and his blasting certificate, he was hand-picked to study mining engineering at Wits University, on a bursary the company had for its employees.

At the School of Mines he was thrown deep into a world he hardly knew existed. A world he had been cocooned from, throughout his childhood. For the first time in his life, he found himself sharing space with young black men and women, his age, who were equally hungry for success and equally capable of achieving it. He had to share this space, not only in lecture halls, but also at Men's Residence where he stayed, and on the sports fields. In his first year, he had taken a keen interest in soccer, under the influence of his roommate, Thabo, a soccer fanatic and striker with a sharp eye for the goal posts.

It was Thabo who gave him his Sotho nickname, Motho Fela. Thabo, in keeping with his name, found humour in almost everything. His jovial approach to life helped him master challenges that were too heavy for most other boys his age. As a first year student, he was to share a double room, with a white youngster. Instead of running from this strange, new experience, he chose to embrace it and make it work.

"After this first week that I have spent with you, here in OC37, I am now ready to give you a name, as a sign that you and I are now brothers. From today onwards, I will call you Motho Fela. You see, my brother, at first I was not so sure if this would work. I had all sorts of anxieties. I was even scared of you, especially on the first night. I wanted to go back to Prof. Hartvol to ask him to allocate me another roommate, but now I have seen for myself that you are just a human being, *o motho fela*, just like me. We are both boys who came to Jo'burg to study mining. So why complicate it?" Motho Fela felt a lump in his throat, while listening to Thabo's kind words. All he ended up saying was, "Oh bru, what does it mean?" And Thabo explained to him that in Sotho it meant human (Motho) just (Fela), which literally means that he saw him as just a human being. Nothing more, nothing less.

Coconut Oil for Dreadlocks

Motho Fela's name was on everyone's lips at the hostel. It was the name itself; also his dribbling skills in soccer; but what really did it, was the hushed rumours about his involvement with Kholofelo. In 1994 at Wits University, and other universities across the country, there were few black students in engineering, let alone women. If you were a young woman, and black, amongst so many young men, you would be the topic in many discussions going on in canteens, bars, sports grounds, hostels and lecture halls. Now if you crossed the colour line, that would really be pushing it. That's exactly what Kholofelo did. She was very clear about what she was doing. Even though she was not fully in control of what it could potentially lead to, but it was something that she dived into, with her big girl's panties tightly held on.

The black guys would always moan about how much Mandela was now allowing white people to even take their women, while the white women on campus had their heart palpitations up to almost boiling point every time they saw the two of them together. The coloured guys couldn't really be bothered, because they had access to both worlds. The Indian guys did not even know what was going on, and they did not care. All that they cared about was smashing those records at Medical School, in Parktown, and the Commerce Faculty on West Campus.

When Kholofelo came to Wits, she was already aware of what South Africa was in the process of becoming. Through her reading, she had been exposed to Nadine Gordimer's work; Professor

Mazisi Kunene's stories; a bit of Bessie Head and a lot of other African Writer's Series material, including Armah Aykweyi's *The Beautiful Ones Are Not Yet Born*. Her mother had access to a mailing system through the Catholic Church, the Jesuits in Braamfontein near Wits University, that gave her an opportunity to source any piece of literature that she wanted for the shabby school library in their home village in Limpopo. As a girl, in high school, whenever she was free from taking care of home chores like fetching water from the river or collecting firewood, Kholofelo would spend her free time reading. This made her look and sound strange to fellow village girls. They struggled to relate with her. She was curious to find out how that form of alienation would play out at university.

One day Motho Fela managed to sneak into her room at Sunnyside res, late on a Saturday evening, and found Kholofelo snuggly couched in blankets, with her fingers curled around a poetry book, and a coffee mug next to her.

"Hey baby, what are you reading? You hardly noticed me coming in. Your face is buried in this book. What is it?" She pulled her glasses down her nose, and looked at him from above the rim, smiling shyly. "It's Maya Angelou, my love. I don't think you know her". Motho Fela had not heard the name before; it did not even sound South African. He asked her to read him the stanza she was on.

"But a bird that stalks
down his narrow cage
can seldom see through
his bars of rage
his wings are clipped and
his feet are tied
so he opens his throat to sing…"

"Don't you just love it?" She asked him teasingly, knowing very well that he knew nothing of this. Mining boys don't have time for touchy feely stuff.
"Read the passage before that one, maybe it will make sense to me", he said, trying to sound interested.

She knew he wasn't interested, but just wanted a polite way of starting conversation with her, so that slowly but surely they could drift away from this heavy and loaded topic into something more real and more relevant to their life together. She decided to make nothing of that, and carried on sharing.

"A free bird leaps, on the back of the wind

and floats downstream till the current ends

and dips his wing in the orange sun rays
and dares to claim the sky"

"Make sense?", again pulling her spectacles down her nose, while smiling as if saying "I wouldn't be surprised if you were more lost than before". But then Motho Fela asked another simple question, "So, what has this got to do with us?" And she explained the whole concept of a caged bird, and the parallels they could draw, the defying of norms and the status quo, flying out of the cage, to claim the sky as theirs.

He could identify with that.

He picked up a white plastic tube which was lying on her side table, and squeezed it out, and asked her "What's this?" and she told him it was coconut oil, for her hair. It was one of the most important cosmetics items she bought religiously every month. In fact, it was the only fancy thing in her vanity drawer. Village life had moulded her to be simple, yet gracious; which is why she had a presence about her, when she walked into a room. She explained to him how much she wanted to grow her dreadlocks, keeping them neat, and two toned with garish orange tip points. She considered her hair, her crown, and her only real claim to being of royal blood.

Motho Fela was not much of a hair admirer; he would complement her mostly on the beauty of her skin. Even though his motivation came from a good place, he never got it right. This was one subject Kholofelo didn't like much. He would talk endlessly about how much he loved her honey glazed skin, which he claimed, glistened in the afternoon sun. But for Kholofelo that was a non-compliment.

She argued that "...why should black women's skin be referred to in food terms like chocolate, caramel, cinnamon, coffee, mocha or even roasted almond. Why couldn't it be labelled according to its real colour, same as it is the case with white women's skin? In most retail outlets, the cosmetics shelves are labelled beige, tawny or tan".

Every time when she sounded like she was about to blow her top, Motho Fela would simply stop talking, and listen, hoping that one day she will cool down or he will learn more about this world he had got himself into.

The winds of change in South Africa could potentially carry them in any direction in the world, if they wanted to. The dawn of democracy had presented everyone with an opportunity to dream, to imagine and picture themselves living a life free from the shackles of apartheid. On paper, apartheid had been scrapped, but in the hearts and minds of those who had come face to face with its harsh realities, it continued to live on.

On the Face of Virgin Rock

Their life at Wits was segmented into two parts. During the year, they were on campus, and on December holidays, they would be working at the mine as vacation students. The eight weeks on the mine, between December and January, gave them an opportunity to experience their chosen fields, in their real and naked form, while at the same time they got a chance to earn a bit of pocket money for themselves. This happened all the way into final year where they eventually joined the mine as graduates.

There was always one challenge though, which they had to deal with, every time they came back to the mine. They had to go through a gruesome process of assimilation and acclimatization. It took a total of two solid weeks, before one could be welcome back into the underground world of mining. This was a process designed not only for new recruits; it was also for employees who had gone on lengthy leave periods or returning students and officials. It included a full medical examination; first aid training; health & safety awareness and the most dreaded heat tolerance test.

Mine workers called it *motshongolo*, which is *Fanagalo* for stepping up and down, a two hour exercise, used to measure a person's susceptibility to heat. It wasn't a sophisticated anthropometric measurement like body surface-to-mass ratio, percentage body fat, body-mass-index or waist circumference. It was just a simple way for mine officials to see if a person could tolerate heat in the underground working areas.

There were no windows in the Heat Tolerance Test Hall. Temperature was controlled, and would be raised a few degrees every 20 minutes, while the long line of workers would be stepping up and down in unison. The rhythm created a form of much needed camaraderie for the 'returning soldiers'. They would even sing, to make it a pleasant, social experience. But, meneer de Wet, didn't really like the singing part, because he said it made a mockery of his work as the *makulu baas* (big boss) of the HTT Hall. He preferred that people take the test seriously, because it was a matter of life and death for them.

After turning the temperature knob up, he would pour ten litres of water thinly across the floor area. The water would soon evaporate into sweat. It was important to keep the air humid. Virgin rock temperatures in most areas along the Witwatersrand Basin can be as high as 30°C at depths of 2.2km underground, but wet bulb temperatures can get as high as 40°C.

Once in a while, a worker would start feeling dizzy and then eventually pass out; and he would be rushed to the mine clinic across the road. For mining crews who worked the stopes and other confined spaces underground, this was crucial, because if they were heat intolerant, it could lead to fatality. The HTT would last a minimum of two days to a maximum of seven. It would be done from 6am until 8am; afterwards everyone would go home to rest, and come back again the following day.

2. YOUR PAIN IS MY PAIN NOW

No Heat, No Gold

The first real form of money in the world was gold *a la natural*. Before gold there were other bartered goods, such as salt and so on. In its natural state, gold is usually accompanied by silver and other precious metals such as copper, iron and other trace minerals. When you go deep into a gold mine, and proceed from the shaft area into the stopes and get to see the gold reef in its natural form, you will find that even though it is physically bonded with the rock formations and trace minerals around it, it is not yellowish and shiny as it looks in its polished final state. It is dark black charcoal in colour. Then there is naturally occurring gold, which falls into two categories – placer (alluvial) and mountainous (eluvial). It is quite rare that you will hear of prospectors talking about alluvial gold dust, nuggets, flakes, grain or flour that they have found near rivers, these days. In South Africa, most of our gold is now found deep in the belly of the earth. If you want real gold, you better dig deep down.

Gold has a lustre and shine that has fascinated human beings for centuries and centuries. It has physical and chemical properties that set it far apart from the rest of the minerals found on earth. Its ductility allows it to be beaten into extremely thin sheets of gold metal. Its malleability allows it to be bent and shaped into many forms. Its conductivity makes an amazing conductor of electricity. Surprisingly, it is also soluble. It is a relatively soft metal, but it is usually hardened by alloying with copper, silver or other metals. It is a dense metal. The most fascinating fact about gold is that its melting point which is 1065^{0}C.

That is a great deal of heat required for gold to change into a liquefaction point. Just to put this into context, consider what happens when human bodies are cremated. The cremation oven operates at an optimum temperature of about 760^{0}C to 982^{0}C. The heat typically comes from propane gas. This differs from country to country, and also it depends on the model of the chamber or oven used.

All the sweat, physical strain, dirt, mud, heat, risking of lives is what eventually produces the gold. Without any of this, there would be no gold.

Motho Fela and Kholofelo knew this very well. They were not naïve when they committed to their version of the cross-racial relationship. They knew that the love they wanted with each other, would come at a price. It would be born out of a great deal of pain and suffering. Most of that pain would come from people around them, and it would also come from within themselves as a couple and as individuals. There were a lot of personal transformation processes that were required to happen as well, for their love to prosper. There was going to be a lot of letting go, and letting come, if they were serious about making it work. The level of commitment necessary for all of that was extra-ordinary.

They put a lot of work into their relationship. Every day was an opportunity for them to put one brick, and another, and another. This daily concerted effort made it to grow steadily and strongly. It blossomed even more when they graduated and started working full time at the mine. The years together at university, had helped them to peel off any form of fake and wishful desire to look like a modern liberated couple. They had moved on from focusing on what it would look like to people, but were more inward looking now, focusing on what it felt like on the inside.

One of the first things that Motho Fela did with his first three salary pay-outs was to put away more than half his salary, for him to be able to buy an expensive diamond ring and jewellery for Kholofelo one day. He hadn't worked out the date when he wanted to propose, but in his heart the decision was already made. He wanted it to be perfect. He was ready for a real lifetime commitment with her. Over the years, she had proved to be a reliable partner, an amazing friend and a great companion for him. They had a lot in common, even though it was on different terms. He had learned a lot from her, and through the life they shared together, he really appreciated how much personal transformation it had afforded him. His outlook towards life had been turned upside down, and inside out.

It was that mind set overhaul process that first left him vulnerable and exposed, and then later served as fertile ground upon which he could plant seeds. Their relationship was marred with both pain and pleasure. The pain was mostly exerted from society, from people in their social circles and total strangers who had a lot of trouble comprehending how it could be that a black woman who had made it in life would choose to be involved with a white guy who also seemed to be doing well. It just didn't make sense. Usually the dynamics are that a black guy who has made it in life would be involved with a white woman who had not achieved much really, but because of her whiteness, the black guy would marry her as a trophy wife. They didn't fit any of those societal norms or expectations.

On the first of May, a few weeks before her birthday, Kholofelo asked Motho Fela if they could go to Klerksdorp for some shopping. She wanted to go to Edgars, to pay her clothing accounts, and then later they would drive to the Vaal River for a picnic near the big Viljoenskroon Bridge. Orkney and Klersdorp are two old Western Transvaal towns that are ten minutes apart, serving the big gold mining communities along the N12, more than 160 km on the North-West of Johannesburg. Even though they both stayed in Orkney, she preferred Klerksdorp because it is bigger and has more options for shopping and things to do. He liked the idea, more so because it would give him a chance to go to Sterns quickly, while she was stuck in queues inside her favourite retailer in town, for some window shopping on what was the latest offering on the gold and diamond range of jewellery. And maybe, if time still allowed, he could run across to Musica and see if he could buy the new Bobby McFerrin CD which had just come out, with songs like *Bang!Zoom* and *Freedom is a Voice*. This could really bode well in setting up the mood, for a chilled Saturday afternoon, on the river banks.

"Baby, what were you doing at Sterns? You know, as I was walking out of Edgards, I saw you glued to that big window display. Please don't tell me you want to buy an expensive gold watch, because you know after 25 years of service at the mine, we will get them for free" They both laughed, and he then responded by saying, "as a gold miner, it makes a lot of sense for me to have gold jewellery. Otherwise what's the point?"

Just when they were carrying on with this light hearted conversation, Kholofelo received a phone call, and everyone on that side walk turned around and looked at her, as she pulled out her cell phone. She could see that the call was most probably from a relative because the dialling code showed that it was a Burgersfort number.

She stepped away from him, so that she could speak freely. She was close enough for him to hear that she was speaking to someone from home, because she spoke her home language, SePedi. Even though he didn't understand much of what she was saying, the only thing that kept his jealousy barometer hovering somewhere between 1 bar and zero, was that time and again she would utter words like "*Awa Mama*" which he knew meant whatever it was that her mother was saying, she wasn't excited about it. This was something he had become accustomed to, in those few months that she had started working, but struggled to accept. Every time he tried to ask what she was upset about, after such calls, she would simply say it is Black Tax, and would not bother to explain what that is.

Deeply Rooted and Connected

"Baby what's going on? Why are you crying? What was that call about?" and she carried on crying, wiping her eyes off. Motho Fela offered her his handkerchief. She took it, but didn't use it. She carried on crying. Now everyone was looking at them. He had to do everything in his power not to appear as the one who made her cry. He was aware of how shallow people could be, in judging situations like that, and the kind of immediate conclusions they would draw even though they didn't know the facts. He held her arm gently, and pulled her into the shop next to them, and asked for a glass of water. They gave him, and offered them a seat. The people in that shop noticed that something bad was happening, and they were curious to find out what it was. They started gathering around them. This made her shy, and she just threw herself on his chest and cried even more. He continued comforting her, but the attention from the fast growing crowd was too much. He whispered into her ear that it was better if they stepped out of the shop and go to the car, which was parked not so far from where they were. And she nodded, in agreement. The crowd was left dumb-founded, and didn't know what to do next.

They got in the car, and drove off, back in the Orkney direction. When they had gone past Klerksdorp Technical College and were out of the CBD, she then started muttering a few words, but with difficulty. "It's Uncle Jonas. He is gone" as she wiped her eyes, and she carried on "It was my mother who was calling me"

This was all new to Motho Fela. He really didn't know how to deal with it. He didn't know what the right words would be; what would be appropriate and what would be rude. So he simply held her hand with his left and carried on driving. The picnic didn't seem like a bad idea. It would help calm her down, and maybe give him a chance to understand the cultural details that come with such an event. As she continued talking about what the call was about, one new piece of information seemed even more disturbing to her. Her mother went on to say that because there were going to be some relatives coming over from Pretoria, for the funeral, Kholofelo had to hire a car and drive them there and back.

Again, this was all new to Motho Fela. It spoke of a lifestyle that he had no clue how it really worked, and yet at the same he was becoming a part of it. In that spare of the moment, he just found himself saying, "I am coming with you".

The passing on of Kholofelo's uncle brought her and Motho Fela very close to each other. The Viljoenskroon Bridge is away from all the noise of the Orkney CBD. It is in a picturesque setting, with great sunset views. Chasing sunsets was something they both loved. The calm of the evening air had a soothing effect on Kholofelo. Motho Fela was a hopeless romantic. The symbolism behind the idea of a bridge, and sunsets, were his way of communicating messages that he didn't have much words for. "Tell me about Uncle Jonas. What was he like? Were you guys close?" And she held on to the rails on the bridge, and let her feet hang down, as she sat down facing away from the sun.

"Uncle Jonas was my closest uncle, out of the five that I have, from my father's side of the family. He worked in Jo'burg, and stayed with Zulu people, at the men's hostel in Denver. He was a Truck Driver. When I moved to Wits University for my studies, we got even closer. He would visit me at Res on weekends. Girls at Sunnyside Hall would laugh at me every time he came over. He would come wearing his work clothes, plus his leopard skin vest, a habit I know he had picked up from those Zulu hostel dwellers. You know migrant workers *mos*. They are like that even here at the mine. He would buy me *spatlo*. And bring it with him, and we would eat it together. You know *spatlo* ne?"

"No. What is it?"

"You take a loaf of bread, and cut it into four quarters. You then hollow it out, and stuff it with polony; cheese; atchar and potato chips and then close it up with the bread soft stuff that you had taken out"

"I have had something like that. But it was in Durban, and it was a bit different. They call it *Bunny Chow*. "

"No man, it's not that. But anyway, as I was telling you, Uncle Jonas was five years younger than my father. Between them is my aunt, the one we met when we went to the Market Theatre in Braamfontein, for Mbongeni Ngema's *Asinamali*. He denounced all his royal privileges in the village, and chose to come eke out a living for himself in the city of gold, away from family drama and heritage disputes. My father does not like that story, but I will tell you anyway. It is still in the courts, and for us as a family we are not allowed to talk about it with *batho fela* (the general public) like you. I will only tell you the little that I know, and some of it has been on the public domain anyway. Back in the late 1800s, Mampuru the 2nd , son of BaPedi King, Sekwati the 1st, was executed by the Transvaal Republiek on 22 November 1883 after being convicted of murdering, a year earlier, on 13 August 1882 Kgoši Sekhukhune the 1st, his brother and rival to the Bapedi Marota throne. For over a century now, these feuds over the crown of the BaPedi Marota Kingdom have resulted in never ending legal battles right up to the courts, which could potentially solve the question of whose lineage has the legitimate claim to the throne. It has divided our family big time, for well over a hundred and twenty years."

"That was barbaric. How could human beings do something like that to fellow human beings, and still call themselves educated and civilized?", and then he took her hand and said, "Baby, I just want to be with you. I was serious when I said I am coming with you. I want to be there for you emotionally, and support you. It wouldn't be right if you went through all of this alone."

"Are you listening to yourself? Where will you sleep? What will I tell my parents? What will everyone say?"

Then he put his left arm around her, over the shoulders, as they were now both sitting on the edge of the bridge and had their feet hanging down over the water. They talked about what they were going to be doing for the rest of the weekend, and even concocted a plan on how Motho Fela's *ubuntu* (humanness) offer was going to work, in practical terms. As the sun kissed the plains of *Bokone Bophirima* (North West), they both stood up, dusted themselves off and jumped in his Double-Cab Isuzu *bakkie*. The plan that they had come up with, involved her younger brother, Thabang, who was studying at Pretoria University. He would be 'the wool they would pull over their eyes'. They then drove back, through Orkney town, all the way past the taxi rank, to Milton Avenue. He dropped her off at the commune in 23 Chesterton and managed to get to his place in time to spend thirty minutes or so watching TV, with the guys in the hall downstairs.

The Bee Keeper's Generosity

"Baby I have good news for you. I just called my father just now. I asked him if he could let me use the family microbus Kombi over the weekend. He said yes, on condition that I would go and fetch it from home and take it to Agenbach Motors in Klerksdorp for a service." Kholofelo jumped for joy, and wanted to hug him, but then didn't, because all the recent graduates who had been booked into the Training Centre for that week's Assertiveness Course, had started arriving and she didn't want unnecessary attention.

This was good news indeed. It meant, after the day's training they could take his *bakkie*, and drive to Fochville together. Lucky enough there was a chance that they could knock off early, at around 14h00, if they behaved themselves especially in the afternoon session. They could be in Klerksdorp minutes before Agenbach Motors closed at 18h00.

"So baby, how about we call them, and let them know that we would like to book in the microbus for a service, but because of time constraints, we might have challenges getting there on time?" They did that. But there was one more thing they still had to figure out. How were they going to get to his parent's house together?

The rest of the Day 1 training centre activities went well, without much drama. Mnr Mostert was pleased with them, and decided to give them the afternoon off, with a case study they had to work on individually as home work. But for the two love birds, this gave them even more time to take care of all their logistical pressures comfortably. They wasted no time. They drove off from the training centre, turning right at the T-junction, towards West Vaal Hospital, all the way past the rugby stadium, and in no time they were on the N12, on the other side of Khuma in Stilfontein heading towards Potchefstroom.

Driving together, on long and short road trips, was something they had gotten used to. It always gave them a chance to connect on an even deeper level, and also to start building some strengths on how to handle hostile people they came across wherever they went. Modernity had been rather slow to reach this particular corner of South Africa. There were still a lot of taboos; prejudices and buffoonery type of social attitudes. Potchefstroom is very close to the AWB headquarters in Ventersdorp. The *Afrikaner Weerstandsbeweging*, with its populist leader still at the helm, even though he was disgraced since he fell off his horse, is still a formidable force around there. You have to keep looking behind your back when walking in the streets of Potchefstroom. So they thought it was prudent to just drive right through town, and only stop when they got to the Zenex Garage in Fochville, where they had to implement their plan of how they were going to reach Motho Fela's home.

"We have two options. I want you to tell me which one you think is going to suit you best. It's either I leave you here in the garage's restaurant, and I get you some steak and kidney pie and a cool drink, while me and Frikkie, the manager of the shop, go home to fetch the microbus, or, you come with us but sit at the back of the *bakkie*. We'll tell my dad that you are just some woman we gave a lift to, at the garage, because you had told us you were going to Klerksdorp." She chose the second option. She wanted to see her future parents-in-law. She was curious what Motho Fela might look like in his old age one day. Also, the adventure was exhilarating for her. So, why not?

Mr du Toit senior was not much of an old man. Kholofelo could see the energetic young fella in him, still yearning to be out and about. There was a refreshingly fast paced abruptness when he walked around the yard. It was as if the bees he kept were always after him, and he had to walk around briskly to confuse them. Or that little fella inside him wanted to jump out and denounce any sanguine resilience and be himself all over again, always keeping busy and curious about almost everything he came across. While Mrs du Toit, on the other hand, had a resigned look, the one of someone who appeared to have given in to how much life had taken out of her and was no longer fighting to get any of it back. Her slightly hunched back and a fringe of grey-white hair in her mottled scalp, suggested that she was a bit older than her husband, which she wasn't. She was in fact five years younger than him.

Motho Fela got the kombi. Exchanged a few quick niceties with his parents, and hopped in his bakkie, while Frikkie drove the microbus. They dropped Frikkie off at Zenex. Kholofelo then took over Motho Fela's *bakkie*, and Motho Fela switched across to the kombi, so that they could drive back to back following each other non-stop all the way back on the N12, to Klerksdorp. The rest of the day went fast, and so did the next few days at the Number One Training Centre.

Certificate of Attendance

"Good morning everyone. Welcome to the Number One Training Centre. Today is our last day for this Assertiveness Course. For us to finish off on a high note, I want you to re-introduce yourselves, one by one, in no particular order. Tell us what your other name is; besides the one that we know already and share with us 'what is that one thing that your colleagues never discovered about you, even though you have been together for the whole week'. Who wants to go first?"

There was a bit of excitement in the room, and everyone was looking at everyone, checking who would be brave enough to be the first one to break the ice. So the skinny Coloured guy, with freckles all over his face and a gold tooth, who was sitting on the left tip of the U sitting formation, stood up and cleared his throat.

"My real name is Shaun Oliver. I am actually not from around here. I know most of you assumed that I am from Doringkruin or something. I am a Western Cape import. When I was a kid, growing up in Elsiesriver in Cape Town, my parents sent me to a Catholic boarding school, so that I could be away from gangsters and drugs. One of the first things I did in my first week there was to sneak into the convent's swimming pool because I was curious about the real lives of those penguin look-alike nuns who taught us at St. Mary's. I really loved the time we had together this week. You might have called me *Bra Fear Fokol*, because I am that brother who is afraid of nothing and no one, but from now on just call me Shaun. "

Everyone clapped hands, and even whistled rather loudly for a formal session like that, but before *Bra FF* could even sit down,

Kenny stood up because he just could not afford to have anyone outshine him. But unfortunately, he couldn't say anything.

Three people walked in. And the fun stopped. It was Motho Fela, with two ladies – one Indian and the other one white. This presented a few challenges immediately. Firstly for Kenny, because he was now interested in finding out where Motho Fela was going to sit. Secondly, for Kholofelo who had been wallowing in the 'I am the only woman in here today' madness. And finally, for everyone else who was now thinking maybe they had to clear up spaces in between them, and make room for the two ladies who were now walking in.

While Mnr Mostert loved the energy mix, and the new dynamics which were now playing out, he was concerned that there would be a lot of drama during the day.

Diversity brings with it a lot of direct and indirect challenges. Only a skilful facilitator can cut through all the fluffy stuff, and bring everyone in and focus them on the main objectives for the day. The idea that Johan Mostert had managed to advance throughout the week, was that learning is not one-directional. It is a multi-directional experience. He also didn't conduct his sessions in a top-down flow, because he knew how quickly that wears him off. He paced himself, and used his energy reservedly so. For that to happen, he had designed the sessions in such a way that the floor was open for all attendees to participate in the generation of knowledge.

A participatory learning process allows for a subversive learning experience. Knowledge should not be the exclusive reserve of the facilitator. Everyone should be made to see themselves as worthy of imparting valuable information; sharing credible knowledge and contributing meaningfully to everyone's growth.

As for Kholofelo, on the other hand the main thing on her mind was how disappointed she was at how the Head of Training, Mr

Peter Patterson, had declined her application for taking the week off, on Monday, when she went to his office to tell him that a family member had died. His words still played out in her head, "But you know the mine policy regarding bereavement" said Patterson, as he loosened his thick maroon branded tie, while looking for the remote to turn the air conditioner a few degrees cooler.

"You are only allowed two days off, if a member of your immediate family has died. The way I understand you, this guy was an extended family member. The policy makes no provision for what happens in such cases. I am afraid you will have to make your own plans, with your own free time. If you decide to leave, regardless of what I have just told you, I will book you AWOL – absent without leave. Do we understand each other?" All she said was "yes sir." A tear dropped from one eye, and she walked out of his office.

At lunchtime everyone else walked across to 1A Milton Avenue, to *Ma de Beer's* canteen, for some mince-meat mixed with raisons, served with spaghetti, and sprinkled with grated cheese, while Kholofelo stayed behind to make a few last minute calls to confirm pick up points with her 'relatives' whom she had to collect in Pretoria, on their way to Burgersfort that afternoon. *Ma de Beer*, or *Madipere* (her Sotho nickname, given to her by the guys who could not pronounce her Afrikaans surname, instead likening it to what it sounded more like in Sotho, which literally means is Mother of Horses), was famous for her culinary variety that was reminiscent of a typical old Western Transvaal farm house, especially the deserts – *melktert* (milk tart with cinnamon) or *koeksisters* (plaited pastries that are steeped in syrup and sometimes dusted with coconut). Her food joint was very popular, because it offered many hungry souls a home experience away from home.

When they came back from lunch, Mnr Mostert was ready to hand out their certificates of attendance. This was something Kholofelo was not particularly excited about, because such a certificate just confirms where you have been and what you were busy with. It doesn't give any indication of your competence level on the subject matter. She felt that it was a total waste of time. She had better things to do that week; things that really mattered to her and her family back in Limpopo.

3. LIVING IN TWO WORLDS

The Harangue

Motho Fela's constant inner dialogue allowed him to start doing the work required to master the demands and challenges of living in many worlds simultaneously. He exerted most of his energies on inner conversations with himself, instead of trying to master the outer world. Conflicting thoughts and ideas would attack him sometimes, leaving him at odds, and lonely. Sometimes, when he was in Kholofelo's world, he would pretend that he was happy - though he knew he didn't fit in. Then he would drift into his own world, a new world he had created for himself where only he resided, which could be cold and scary. He often wondered where he belonged. Being unhappy in his own private world and lonesome in Kholofelo's world left him in a label free, transitional state of identity. Even though Kholofelo tried to introduce him to her old friends and relatives, he struggled to fully be a part of that world. Their old memories were new to him. Their jokes and general sense of humour was sometimes not funny. But then there was no turning back. He had made his life choice. He had to embrace his new world that he was growing into. He was the happiest when it was just the two of them. If he had things his own way, they would just block everyone off, and live alone. Unfortunately that's not how life works.

Finishing early at the training centre meant they could walk across to Motho Fela's place, at 1A Milton Avenue, where the microbus was parked. The mechanics at Agenbach Motors in Klerksdorp, had done a good job servicing it, a few days earlier. When they fetched it from Fochville on Monday, Motho Fela's father had warned him that water was not flowing properly to the radiator and the thermostat was not working, which made it overheat sometimes. He didn't mind the maintenance costs, if it meant a smooth road trip to a world he longed to visit. He made sure he remembered everything he had been told, so that if the problem persisted, he knew exactly what to do. "My *bru*, you might have more than one headache here" said Pitso, the mechanic, when he had finished doing the diagnostics on the microbus, while Motho Fela and Kholofelo looked on. "Obviously the cooling system is compromised. I will first check the cylinder head gasket. We'll do a compression leak test. From there we'll look at the hose between the radiator and the engine. It's also quite possible that the thermo-switch in the radiator is failing which is causing intermittent cooling fan failure. I recommend replacing it, doing a coolant flush and then we can go for a spin around town, maybe up the Joubertina stretch of road." These words had stuck with him the entire week. He had driven it around a few times, and he was happy about how it was handling. His anxiety levels were down, but there were no guarantees.

They had packed everything up, including Motho Fela's 20 litre cooler box. He didn't have much in there, besides ice cubes, fizzy drinks, Lion Lager and Kholofelo's cranberry juice. He promised her that he would not touch a single drop of alcohol while driving.

When he told S'bu, his closest friend at work, that he was going to the funeral that weekend, S'bu advised him to take a bottle of brandy or whisky, for the *after tears*. He explained how much Kholofelo's uncles and other village men would appreciate it, even forget that it was a time of mourning. He bought two bottles of Oude Meester, one Klipdrift brandy plus two Smirnoff Vodka for good measure.

He wasn't sure what to expect when he got there. First, he had never been introduced officially to Kholofelo's family. They didn't even know that she had a boyfriend, let alone a white one. Second, it was his first time to spend a weekend immersed deep in the culture, customs and traditions of rural black society.

As they drove off the single quarters, turning right into the West Vaal hospital road, Kholofelo initiated some small talk. He responded with one word answers. He was deep in thought. This continued until they got to Pretoria. Kholofelo noticed that he was distant and chose not to bother him. Instead, she put on some Eryka Badu.

The Journey of Identity

The plan they had concocted over their picnic on Saturday, was that Motho Fela would be introduced as Thabang's friend from university. To compensate for the fact that he was much older, they were going to say that he was a junior lecturer in the Zoology and Botany Department; a specialist in apian studies. This was a safe bet, in case some overzealous village inquisitor asked questions. Motho Fela could tell them all about bee behaviour. Though Thabang knew about Motho Fela, they had never met.

Thabang did not live up to his reputation of being tardy. They found him waiting with his bag at the Shell garage, ready for him to go. "Eh Thabang, this is Motho Fela, *ke yena motho waka*, he is my person." said Kholofelo,

Because of the age gap between them, Thabang had to show some respect. He leaned forward, and shook hands with his future *swaer* (brother-in-law). Motho Fela seemed welcoming, and that was encouraging.

The first thing Thabang noticed when he opened the boot, to put his bag in, was the cooler box. This was going to be an exciting road trip. There were other items back there. Motho Fela is a light traveller. Kholofelo is quite the opposite. She is that person who will pack three bags of different sizes for a weekend long trip, and when it is time to go, she would open all of them up again, making sure she had not forgotten anything. Two or three times along the way, she would ask, "where did I put my makeup bag?" or "do you have any idea if I put my coconut oil in the toiletry bag?" All of which never really made sense to Motho Fela, because, although she carried all of these items that were intended to enhance her beauty and promote her attractiveness, she hardly used any of it. Lip gloss was always more than enough, especially on days she would go underground or like on this trip where she was expected to show up at home with a *doek* (head wrap) and a long skirt, preferably black in colour.

This road trip was their longest trip together, and it was the first time they had to share the experience with family members and her relatives. There was a lot for both of them to look forward to. Road trips are also a trip of the mind, and of the heart, when you consider the different movie scenes playing out in your head, as you project into what is most likely to happen; the constant backward and forward motion lending a cinematic effect, with a built-in narrative paced by what is pumping out of the speakers. The ever changing scenes, the dips and dives of terrain, all become a screen for your imagination.

They took the N4 towards Pretoria East, so that they could drive through Witbank and Middelburg, and head towards southeast Limpopo. But first, they had to take a short left into Mamelodi, a township hardly twenty minutes east of Pretoria CBD, to pick up the three aunties that Kholofelo's mother had asked her to bring with. They were the reason why in the first place she needed a bigger car, and why Motho Fela had been thoughtful enough to ask his parents for the microbus. To make everybody's life easier, she had called them earlier that day asking them to take a taxi out of the township and wait for them at that big traffic circle near the highway. And that's exactly what they did. They had lots of luggage. Motho Fela noticed that they all had blankets with them, and for him, this took his mind to what the sleeping arrangements were going to be like at Ga-Mohlala.

They did not dwell on the fact that Motho Fela was white. It was a bit of a surprise, and they were concerned about how they were expected to speak English all the way to Limpopo and back. They preferred Afrikaans, because that's what they were fluent in, from their work in the suburban kitchens where they were as domestic workers. For Kholofelo and Thabang Afrikaans was not a language they would speak. They had forgotten it when they finished high school where they had learned it as a second language. After the introductions were done, and pleasantries exchanged, and were now back on the highway about to get to the first toll gate, Aunty

Betty started giving them what felt like it was going to be a lengthy and a heavy lecture on ancestral beliefs and customs, but turned out to be much lighter than that.

"You know *bana baka* (my children), our presence here in this car means that all our ancestors are also present here with us. They brought us together, and they are going to protect us on this trip that we are taking with each other now. They are alive in us. Every time we talk, share a smile, all the generations of our ancestors, they smile too. Even *swaer* Jonas is here with us. What we are doing here, we are not just doing it for ourselves but for the generations to come. The river of life never stops flowing. It continues forever. This is my way *bana baka* to say thank you for arranging this."

The trip was supposed to take three hours, but time and again they would stop, at garage stores for chilly bites, Motho Fela's favourite *biltong* variety, or to fill up, it ended up taking five hours. This gave them enough time to get to know each other, to prepare for the weekend. All sorts of motion pictures were playing in Motho Fela's head. One minute he was thinking about what would happen in the morning, when they woke up. Where would he shower? What time would they be expected to wake up? What would they eat for breakfast? What sort of village was Ga-Mohlala? And, when they noticed that he was drifting away in thought, they would switch over to SePedi, their language, so that they could talk freely about the funeral arrangements. Revered cultural events, like funerals are handled with much secrecy and mystery, caught between staunch Christian beliefs and ancient African tradition and idiom.

Bastions of Male Privilege

As they approached Steelpoort, Motho Fela took his first breath of dusty, dry Sekhukhuneland air. In that moment, he knew he was in for an experience that would be branded into his memory. The weekend would shape his understanding of his future wife's world but also get him to recalibrate his appreciation of the world her roots were anchored in. The sun had set, but its colours, hues and shades were still traceable on the mountain tops. This was an experience that was not just delightful for the eye, but it engaged all the other senses as well. This sensual assault involved the sounds of boys driving cattle back to their enclosures at home, the smell of cow dung and thick pollen in the air. The effect it created was majestic. The homesteads and compounds that dotted the plains everywhere he turned his eye to, presented a quintessential African village experience, with silhouettes of thatched *rondavels* against an ochre-painted sky. Whilst the trees, shrubs, rockery and landscape made for a traditional Limpopo feel, Motho Fela felt a sudden sense of freedom, an awakening of a sort. It was as if he was living the words of Maya Angelou from that poem Kholofelo had read to him back at university. His wings and feet were surely not clipped anymore, and he was free to take to the skies, and fly high.

When they finally arrived, he said a prayer, grateful for that the successful trip – the microbus never overheated; the *aunties* were pleasant and even slept along the way; but more importantly, they were safe.

As they got off the microbus, the first thing he noticed was the number of people roaming around the yard, 80% men. They were clad in dark coloured blazers and jackets that had seen better days. They spoke in low tones. Almost all of them wore, pinned to their lapels, a silver star against a green piece of cloth. Thabang explained that this denoted their membership of the Zionist Christian Church, reportedly the biggest African-initiated church in Southern Africa.

Motho Fela was not religious, but agnostic. His family subscribed to Protestant Afrikaans traditions which can be traced back to the French Huguenots, Calvinist refugees, who settled in the Cape in the late 1600s after fleeing from persecution by Louis XIV who had revoked a law protecting religious tolerance – the Edict of the Nantes.

As they settled in, going from hut to hut, members of the family and village mourners, all women, came to greet them. They were welcomed with warm hands. This would be followed by a question, "… *ke mang o* (now who is this)." They brushed it off, saying that this is Thabang's friend from school" But the facial expressions said they didn't buy it, they knew there was a bigger story. Some villagers simply thought that since this was a royal funeral, strange things could be expected. Some expected the media to show up, especially on Saturday morning. Anything was possible.

The men in the cattle enclosure had just finished slaughtering an ox and two goats, in keeping with custom, and the meat was being carried into the main hut for roasting on the coal for supper. It seemed like a lot of work. Motho Fela did not offer assistance, fearing that it might offend cultural beliefs and customs. He had to exercise a certain restraint, not just now but throughout the weekend. He fought the temptation to pull out his camera whenever he saw something worth capturing on film.

While the women were quietly tucked away indoors, men of all ages were now congregated in groups, drinking traditional home brewed beer, some of them getting a bit loud and unruly.

Thabang had arranged for some of his schoolmates from the village to visit with him and Motho Fela, 'his friend from university'. Not all of them came. On weekends, people in the villages are torn by invitations to happy occasions like weddings and birthday parties. You don't want to neglect your friends in their time of sorrow, but a bit of fun would not kill anyone. What made the number of invitations overwhelming sometimes, for rural folk, is that migrant workers, labourers, and white collar officials, based in big cities like Johannesburg and Pretoria, would come to the villages to host events. You cannot host a traditional ceremony in the cities. The houses don't have *umsamo* (the sacred space reserved for traditional rituals).

Only two of Thabang's friends showed up. He was surprised to see that one of his friends was limping on his left leg. "And now?" said Thabang, pointing at his friend's leg. "*Eyi mona*, accident" said his friend, pulling up a trouser leg part to show him. "We were driving back from a party in Polokwane, in my father's car. All of us were drunk, and I lost control of the car and it rolled over into a ditch. Luckily no one died, but I now have a prosthetic leg. So I wanted to warn youngsters about our drinking problem in South Africa, that's why you see this tattoo at the back of the good leg – "one foot in the grave".

Motho Fela was gaining insight into the rural psyche. They were not as backwards as he had been led to believe. There is a paradox playing out in the villages. One minute you see girls on the compound carrying 20 litre buckets of water on their heads, that they have brought from a nearby stream; a minute later two girls show up wearing crop tops and tight fitting jeans or mini-skirts. This would immediately get a random uncle worked up, who would shout to them saying "go back to wherever you come from and change into more respectable clothes. Don't you see that we have a funeral here? Your skirts are so short I thought they were belts. *Sepelang*! (go away)".

This was a rude awakening for him to see how sexist culture and custom can be, and also how within that practice there was a thin disguise of misogyny. Women are expected to be passive, soft spoken, polite and dress up in a way that is approved by men. Those who violate patriarchal norms and expectations are seen as morally objectionable. Statements could be heard like *"akere lena le di rights"* meaning just because you now have rights does not mean you can think of changing how things are done in traditional spaces.

Glorified Migrant Workers

Very early Saturday morning, around 2AM, an hour before Thabang's alarm was set to go off, there were footsteps and loud voices outside the hut where he, Motho Fela and one of the cousins had spent the night. It was time for everyone in the compound to wake up, and get ready for the big day ahead. Funerals start early, and finish an hour or two after sunrise. This allows everyone to attend to pressing errands in town. As if the noise was not torturous enough, there was someone at the door, "Knock-knock guys, open up. Your water is ready". It was Kholofelo with a big plastic tub of lukewarm water for Motho Fela to bath in. There was no time for lighting a candle, or to exchange niceties. Her chores for the day had already started, and as one of the senior girls in the family she had a long list of things to do before the sun was up. A few minutes later, she was back with more water, now for Thabang. Before she went back to get water for the cousin, who was still asleep, Motho Fela threw her the microbus keys, asking her to get his toiletry bag and his black jacket. Just like that, the quietude of his morning had been hijacked. His romantic ideas of enjoying the sunrise and serenity of village life, were dashed. He had longed for it since the idea of a weekend in Limpopo first crossed his mind. He loved sunrises mainly because in mining, work starts so early. It had promised to be a rare occasion to witness this great feat of nature, where as the sun rises, brilliant colours seep into the sky, saying goodbye to the darkness and hello to the morning brightness.

Motho Fela finished washing up, got dressed, and stepped outside. To his amazement, there were cars everywhere. There were two buses as well, parked outside the compound, near the main gate. Many people had arrived overnight, probably relatives and family friends from afar. Strangely, the windows of most cars were misted up. There were people inside. They had slept there the whole night. The same was the case with the buses. People were still wrapped up snuggly in their multi-coloured blankets. The number plates told of the province they had travelled from. Besides those with an L for Limpopo at the end, there were a lot of GPs probably from Pretoria and Johannesburg, plus MPs from nearby towns in Mpumalanga. The gravity of the event became apparent to Motho Fela. On what had been open space in the middle of the yard, was now a huge marquee for the ceremony. It was still relatively dark outside, but people didn't seem troubled by it. They found their way around quite easily.

While he stood outside, enjoying the pollution-free, village air, Thabang called him back in. He wanted to brief him on what was going to happen, from little details about breakfast to serious matters about the funeral procession and its protocol. He also wanted to warn him about using his camera. It was okay to take pictures, as long as he did not do so excessively and did not do it in full awareness of the family elders, because they would kick him out. As they spoke, he occasionally got sprinkled by water from Thabang's cousin who was naked in the tub two meters away. Although the setting was different, it wasn't strange to have another man bathing in front of him. The mine change house exposure had prepared him. He was okay with it.

"*Felo*, make sure you serve these city boys some tea before it gets busy," a husky woman's voice, instructed Kholofelo outside. Thabang told Motho Fela that it was his mother. Her voice sounded like that probably because of all the speaking, in thin night air, and her throat was most likely irritated. It sounded like Kholofelo's voice, minus the rough bit. This made him anxious. It was real; he was going to meet his future mother-in-law.

As instructed, within minutes tea was served, on a tray covered by a beautifully decorated white net to keep the flies away. It came with sumptuous warm scones and homemade jam. Kholofelo's mother felt it was an important courtesy for the white visitor Thabang had brought home with him. She wanted him to feel comfortable and well taken care of, so that he would go back to Pretoria and tell his friends how hospitable rural people had been in Sekhukhuneland.

At exactly 5AM, a low sounding horn bellowed out, for a minute or two, and as it grew louder, deep modulated acapella men's voices accompanied it. This made everyone want to step out of their huts and join in the 'performance'. It signalled that official funeral procedures had begun. Leading the procession was a tall, ungracefully thin middle aged man, with a well cut fox skin over his shoulders. In his hands, was a long twisted kudu horn, which had been hollowed out and converted into a traditional musical instrument. Behind him were about twenty senior men wearing dark coloured shades of black and brown. The first four were poll bearers, followed by a praise singer, who was reciting the clan's praise names and poems. While the singing carried on, Motho Fela stood outside. He saw the large casket which was adorned with fresh cow hide, probably the one slaughtered the previous day, to showcase Uncle Jonas's seniority in the family. There was a gap between the first group of chief mourners, and the second. That batch was much larger. The men in it were not just singing; some were engaged in small talk while miming along. At the back of the procession were the women, each covered in blankets over their shoulders, with head wrap on and very long skirts. Those who joined in would first check which social rank was placed where in the windy procession. It didn't proceed straight into the marquee, but snaked around the compound into the gate of the cattle enclosure before it went into the tent.

When finally it reached the tent, everyone took their places – men on chairs, women and children on the floor. Lucky enough there was carpet covering the entire area of the marquee. In front, facing the mourners, were three priests and an interpreter. The interpreter had amazing language skills. He could speak SePedi; isiNdebele and English with flair and ease, which bode well for the mixed group of people that attended the funeral. Everyone was impressed with him, except for one blunder he made at the end when he said "*Go Well, Go Shell*". People turned their heads towards each other, asking themselves if he had been given the job because of his oil and gas connections. English translations were provided, not for Motho Fela or the media, but so that city dwellers would feel that the funeral was of a high standard. The accent didn't matter. They could live with 'politics' pronounced '*polo ticks*' or, 'municipality' being '*money sea pality*' or common words treated like compound words, butchered down to strange stems such as '*participate*' becoming '*party see pate*'. While they didn't mind partying after the formal proceedings were over, it was too early in the day and inappropriate to hint that a huge *After Tears* had been planned.

The Yawn of Democracy

Around 9AM all the formal processes had been carried out. The much dreaded drive to the cemetery did not happen. Uncle Jonas was buried on the outer ring of the yard, next to the cattle enclosure, with all his forebears.

They all came back from the gravesite, and started queueing for breakfast. All over the compound, there were groups of people eating and young girls serving them, walking briskly from group to group with trays in their hands, making sure all of demands were met. If there was an uncle who wanted cold water with ice, it was promptly provided. If there was a distant relative who complained that there was too much tea in his sugar, another cup would be served right away. This was normal, and no one thought of it as too much for the girls, except for Motho Fela. He thought the girls were used as cheap labour. "Why didn't they hire a catering company? They are royalty, aren't they?, he asked himself. But then he could not share such thoughts with anyone, not even Kholofelo.

Late afternoon, as the crowds started to disperse, new informal groups began forming. It was mostly youth who had not attended the funeral, assembling under the acacia trees outside the gate where the buses had been parked overnight. They had cooler boxes and camp chairs and had opened their boots, to play music while partying away. As the drinking spree started, the noise levels grew louder. Every ten minutes or so, there would be that mindful girl who would ask the owner of the car to turn the volume down. These were youngsters who worked in local cities and towns like Polokwane, Mokopane, Lebowakgomo and Marble Hall, who only come home on weekends. Visiting home gives them an opportunity to brag and boast about their material accumulations since the dawn of the new dispensation. The material comforts that they enjoyed gave them access to the good life, and thought they were now free to do whatever they wanted with their money.

"You know it's May now, and I have been a gold member of Virgin Active for five months already. I expected that by now my beer belly would be gone. Nothing has changed. Instead, the more time goes by, the fatter I become. Maybe now it's time I go there in person, and find out what's really going on with my membership", said one young man in his early twenties, in a slurred voice. They had no plans to stay sober. By sunset they were plastered, and had completely forgotten what the occasion was. As it got darker, the groups grew bigger. It was as if some of them were nocturnal, because coming out at night meant people could not see who they were and what they were really up to.

First Moment to Pause

1. What battles did you have to fight for you to get to where you are now?
2. Who were you before the people around you told you who they wanted you to be?
3. How does your persona shift when you find yourself in unfamiliar territory, dealing with stressful circumstances?
4. What is your tolerance for heat (pressure), in your life and at work? What key competencies do you need to flourish in such situations?
5. How do you create a safe space and show sympathy for others, when they share their pain with you? How do you support them?
6. What meaning do you attach to things that happened in the past? How is the past serving you now? What are you willing to let go?
7. How much of what you refer to as 'your world', is really your world?
8. What is your level of comfort when dealing with people who are your psychological opposites, who do not see life the way you do?
9. In which way would you say you have been a caged bird all these years?
10. What kind of an eco-system would be necessary for you to rise up to the best version of yourself, sharing love and kindness?

SECTION 2: MIRROR (VISION)

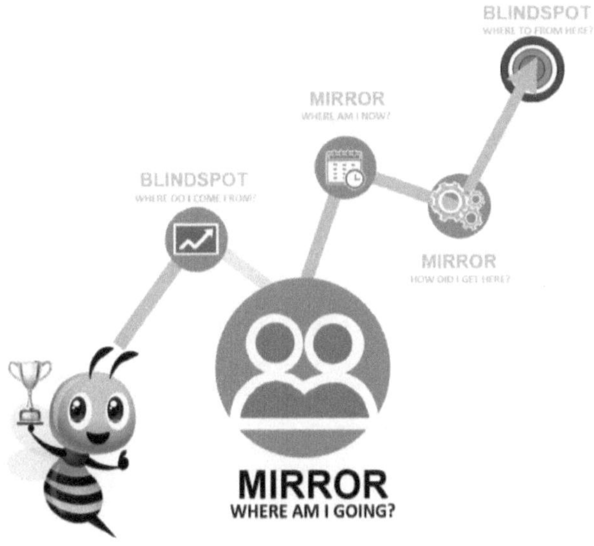

"The most authentic thing about us is our capacity to create, to overcome, to endure, to transform, to love and to be greater than our suffering."

Ben Okri

4. BOUNCEBACKABILITY

Transforming Pain into Productive Energy

Emotionally secure individuals do not fall from heaven, fully equipped to handle any form of pain, suffering, grief, disappointment or shock.

They are a product of years and years of iterative processes framed by cultural teachings that promote collective identity, sharing of pain, crying together, spiritual expression and the pooling in of individual strengths into one big collective emotional bank account.

This becomes a resource they can always draw from, a coping mechanism, or a safety net to handle adversity. In such structures the main emphasis is on the development of warm social relationships, creating strong ties with extended family, which then breeds closely knit community bonds. No one is encouraged to be a lone wolf. Individual identity is derived from the identity of the collective. In this way individuals are driven by the ambitions and goals of the collective.

Wealth, therefore, is not defined by your material possessions, but by your ability to give care and take it from others. Generosity in all its forms is the glue that binds societies together.

Kholofelo was brought up in that system. But she was also exposed to another world, one with different beliefs about wealth, material and making a contribution in life. This was the case for most other youngsters in her peer group. The trappings of city life dissociated them from their true identity.

From her childhood all the way to the weekend of her uncle's burial, she was still clay, for shaping and moulding.

The same was true for the young girls Motho Fela saw, criss-crossing the crowds as low cost waiters. They were participating in practical cultural training; an intentional relationship building exercise. As they served food to the elders, they got to meet their aunts, grannies and all other relatives within the clan. They learned who they are; where they come from and how they fit into the cultural spider web. Their responsibilities helped them build confidence, and emotional security. Connectedness wired threads in their hearts and minds. It added to their emotional bank accounts.

As they drove back to Pretoria, and then later on to Orkney, there was not much talking in the car. They didn't even play music. There was no appropriate music to play.

When Motho Fela checked his rear view mirror he noticed that even the Mamelodi aunties were sleeping. It was time for him to carry on a conversation with himself. His thoughts were trying to settle on an accurate interpretation of what he had witnessed. It was all new to him, and it didn't make much sense. He had many questions.

He knew this experience would allow him to connect with Kholofelo on a more meaningful level. Before the funeral, his view of her culture and customs was condescending. He was not aware of it, but it was there in the colour of his words and the tone of his speech.

While they were still at university, two weeks after they first met, he asked her "why do you people make funerals such a big deal? Why do you spend so much money on them while there is so much poverty around you?"

But as time passed his attitude morphed gradually towards understanding and respect, until he was open. Now he thought, "it must be really exciting to be connected to all your family members, at such an authentic level, without pretences or showmanship".

Thabang, on the other hand. was not asleep, although he looked like he was. "You know I still can't believe Uncle Jonas is gone, forever," he said, breaking the silence. "You know it was hardly a month ago when I last saw him. He had come home for the Easter weekend, and I spent a bit of time with him. He was a great storyteller, and an amazing historian. He told me how much he resisted being appointed as one of *dikgosana*. The idea of serving in the local Tribal Council, dealing with village disputes did not appeal to him."

"What is *Dick Hose Anna*," interjected Motho Fela.

"*Dikgosana* are a council of tribal headmen who lead the communities within a tribal authority. Each person who serves there is referred to as *kgosana*, and together they form *legotla la diKgosana* which is the council. Each one leads about 120 families or so, who are part of a clan. This council then reports to the chief, *Kgosi*. Under him, there are 20 clans here. *Moshate* "

"You should have given me this lecture on our way to Ga-Mohlala, but anyway carry on."

Thabang went on to explain how much his uncle didn't want to be part of the constant conflicts between traditional systems and the new democratic structures. He felt there was duplication; a waste of resources; neither structure served the real interests of the people. There was also overlap in crime prevention duties between the police and vigilante groups in the villages. There was all the secrecy around tribal matters, authority and succession, especially concerning the royal family. He wanted peace, and working in Johannesburg gave that to him.

He didn't like the politicians either, especially the new breed of careerists, whose pockets were never full enough and whose appetite for power could never be satisfied. He told many stories about how they would co-opt traditional leaders into signing deals with big businesses wanting to build on tribal land. In return the politicians ~~got~~ security of their positions. The chiefs would guarantee to mobilise the people to vote for the politicians when election time came.

Deconstruction, Reflection and Construction

Kholofelo only woke up when they stopped in Mamelodi to drop off her aunts. Their luggage had doubled in size. Mostly it was food parcels, in huge plastic containers. "A lot of exchange must have happened back at Ga-Mohlala" mused Kholofelo.

All of a sudden the old ladies were full of life, and had a lot to chat about. The house where they were being dropped off was full of children who had missed their grandmothers, excited about what they had brought them from the village. Return trips from Limpopo Province are accompanied by loads of *avocado, masonja (dried mopani worms) and mango*, depending on the season or the region visited.

Kholofelo only got a chance to speak freely when they were alone in the car, after they had dropped off Thabang, at the University of Pretoria. She knew Motho Fela would have lots to say about what he had seen; what it looked like to him and what his feelings were. Sitting in the front passenger seat now, she could look at him, and engage better. "Soooooo *motho waka* (my person), how was it?" she asked with a broad smile.

Motho Fela shook his head gently sideways, and his face turned bright and said, "weeeeeena (youuuuu)", which short for, "I love how you are leading me into this new world, and appreciate the style and grace you showed throughout the weekend."

Motho Fela was getting the hang of living his life focused more on being instead of doing. Kholofelo had introduced him to the idea; stop, look, think; process things; find meaning in what you are experiencing.

"I would not have learned, if I did not go with you" started Motho Fela. "I think, I'm one lucky bugger. How many white guys my age, here and now in 1998, four years into democracy, do you know of, who have had first-hand experience of the Rainbow Nation promise? Raw and naked?"

"Wait a minute Desmond Tutu, before you carry on, we need to fill up and check that radiator," Kholofelo replied. "We might also need coolant. I don't want us to get stuck on the road. It's been a long week as it is."

They turned off at the next off-ramp and looked for a filling station.

While Motho Fela opened the bonnet, for the petrol attendants to check the water and oil, and let the engine cool down a bit, Kholofelo went into the convenience shop for drinks, *biltong*, chocolate and wine gums.

"This has been a *lekker* (very nice) week. Thanks babes for this amazing experience. Yes, there is nothing nice about death, but I'm blown away by the opportunity I've just had. I got to take part in a real African funeral. I was there, in person. I didn't read about it in a newspaper or magazine. One day, when I'm an old man, I will tell these stories to my grand-children; *our* grand-children babes."

They carried on reminiscing about the week gone by. The first part of it being the classroom experience and then the last bit of it being the more intense cultural immersion. Motho Fela now had real friends in the village, Ga-Mohlala. He had also made friends with people from there, who were working in Pretoria and Johannesburg. He could relate to them, because they were glorified migrant workers, just like him.

But the most important person he met there, was himself.

As a child and later at Wits, he had learned about the injustices of colonialism and apartheid, how deep the social fractures were and how brutal the scars, but he had no idea how superficial his understanding was. This experience opened his eyes to details that he had been shielded from. It invited a new level of awareness, respect and empathy. His visit had given him a rare opportunity to see for himself how the social fault lines cut through what used to be proud, well-constructed, cohesive and just socioeconomic structures and systems. What he found were pieces of what it used to be, in its former glory. He came away with the strong conviction that African narratives need to be re-storied.

His new awakening elevated his social consciousness. He now wanted to walk the path that would lead him to become a change maker, a challenger of the status quo, a dream weaver, a social justice crusader. He had seen the tangible effects of past injustices - the land and the poverty. He was now more interested in the intangibles: indignity, humiliation, dehumanization, hopelessness, woundedness, anxiety, depression and a lack of ambition. He didn't yet know how it was going to happen, but he knew it had to. He would find a way. He had observed over the first four years of democracy, how politicians talked about social cohesion, but practised a new brand of social control. He didn't want to be a part of something that would coerce and subdue. He wanted substance, depth and human connection.

For the rest of the drive, the emotional load was made easier by the music Kholofelo put into the CD player: Eryka Badu's *On and On* to which she sang along:

I was born under water
With three dollars and six dimes
Yeah, you might laugh 'case you did not do your math
Like one, two, three
The world keeps turning
Oh what a day, what a day, what a day
The man that knows something
Knows that he knows nothing at all
Does it seem colder in your summertime and hotter in your fall?
If we were made in his image, then call us by our names
Most intellects do not believe in God
but they fear us just the same
Oh on and on and on and on!!!

If They Don't Eat, We Won't Sleep

When Motho Fela was back at the mine, on Monday morning, throughout the production meeting and afterwards when all the shift bosses were busy with their underground material orders and scheduling, he noticed that the others kept looking at him. It was as if they wanted him to share how his weekend was, without being brave enough to ask *"so what's it like spending the weekend with darkies?"*

Mnr Koekemoer, the production manager, walked in and wanted to speak to the team. This was unusual, for him to budge in like that, unannounced.

He wanted to talk to them about a possible strike. The union bosses had been talking about it in hushed tones, in corridors and openly at the men's hostel. He had picked up the rumour from, Moonlight Madi, his *pikinin* (a deragoratory term for an assistant). The union was plotting to stage a go slow on June the 19th because they were not happy with their weekend overtime pay and nightshift allowance.

When Mnr Koekemoer had finished his talk, he said "……now, you must all know that I know that some of you are buddies with these people. Some of you even spend weekends with them. But I want you to keep this under wraps. No word about it. We have to prepare for it. And, preparing means we have to plan for the worst. The 19th of every month is measuring day. It's a chance for us as the production team to know exactly how we have performed, and how much bonus we can expect at the end of the month. If this go slow happens, it means there will be no sweepings and no confirmation of how much we advanced in the stopes or how many meters we drilled in the haulages or new ore passes. These people are hungry. We are also hungry. And you know how dangerous a hungry man is. If they don't eat, we won't sleep. We have to protect our bonuses. We have to protect our jobs. Thank you. The rest of you can carry on, but you Gert du Toit, *na my kantoor toe* (to my office)." Motho Fela followed him.

Mnr Koekemoer pulled out a chair for him in his office, and went to sit on the other side of the table. "I want you to do something for me. You see the strike I was telling you all about, could cripple mine production figures for this month. I will suffer, you will suffer and we will all suffer. We do not want that. Here is where you come in. We are entitled to know exactly what they're planning, when, how and who will be doing what and where. Are we clear? I see you as a very important link for us with these people. I want you to make them feel free around you, as they already are, and get them to speak to you about everything. *Alles* (everything). And every day I want you to report back to me. I will make sure you have a good stay in my section, and even arrange for you to be considered for promotion to our new shaft opening up on the other side of the Vaal River next year. Do we have a deal?"

Motho Fela knew exactly how much power Mnr Koekemoer wielded on the mine. He had direct access all the way up to the general manager, Mr Jacob Janaway, who was his brother-in-law. He had married Mr Janaway's younger sister, Claudette. They spent family time on weekends together at his official residence, near the Vaal River Lagoon.

There was no way Motho Fela could refuse this request. He simply said yes, and walked out. It gave him time to absorb the shock of what his superiors really thought of his connection with the labourers on the mine. While the strike was going to have a devastating effect on the mine, he knew that the union's demands were legitimate. He was caught in a dilemma. Capitulating on Mr K was a big 'No, No'.

Nuanced Resilience

Bullying in the workplace is rife. It's worse when mixed in with narcissist behaviour. Motho Fela did not have time for any of that. While on the outside he gave the appearance of being non-threatening, of someone Mnr Koekemoer could count on, inside he was hatching a plan to dismantle the toxic mine culture, a system that was slowly swallowing him.

Resisting it directly was not going to work. He had to be diplomatic. The first idea he came up with was to understand both sides thoroughly so as to form an objective opinion. He wanted to take a principled stand. To do that, he had to have all the facts, and not base his decisions purely on hearsay and emotions. He wanted to get the full context. The thing with bullies is that they live in a bubble of fear; when you pierce it, it is a shock to see how empty it really is. He wanted to pierce it, carefully and neatly.

When he finished with his morning paperwork, he went to the change house, and put on his underground, protective work gear. He headed straight to the shaft. At the surface station, he made sure to greet everyone – the mine officials in their white overalls; the engineering crew in their blue hard hats and the material handlers with their Scotch cars loaded with timber. The three decker cage came, and everyone walked into their respective compartments according to rank and mine status. For a change, Motho Fela went into the cage reserved for officials, instead of the general workers' cage as he usually did. He chose to go right to the back, where they wouldn't notice or talk to him. Once the cage started moving, and gaining momentum, as it plunged deep into the mine ,talking became difficult. The ears got blocked because of the increasing pressure, the deeper they went. The noise, from the mechanical systems in action, was not helpful either. Those who talk, during such rides, must have really pressing matters to get off their chests; or they're the peacocks who crave attention and praise. So, to balance the pressure in their ears, they have to keep chewing or gyrating their lower jaw bones.

"There is this new graduate from Wits whose love for chocolate has made him think he can change how things are done here on the mine" said a loud unfamiliar voice, from somewhere near the roller door of the cage. Everyone laughed. "That guy must be nuts" said another voice that Motho Fela did not recognise. "We know guys like that. Those nonsense ideas don't work here" carried on the second guy. The more they spoke, the more anxious he became.

The thing with exclusionist behaviour is that its main aim is to control people, while blaming them for their exclusion. It doesn't see anything wrong with itself. It is self-absorbed, denialist and shallow. Within it, are contradictions, insecurities and narrow-mindedness. To understand it, you need to dig a few layers in.

When they arrived at the 45th level, he elbowed his way out quickly before the On-setter could signal for more descent again. The new section he was now allocated to was on the far east haulage, about 15 minutes' walk from the station. As a rule, when you are not so sure of your direction underground, you follow the water. The drains on the side of walls are sloped in such a way that they let the water flow from the working areas inside the mine to the shaft, where it drains into the collection systems that pump it out. He followed the water backwards, making sure he read the markings on the walls and direction arrows. When he finally got to the waiting room, he found his drilling team ready for him to mark the holes they were going to charge with explosives. They had done all the safety procedures, water and electricity checks.

"Muhle kanjan madoda? (Fanagalo for: Great, how is it guys," greeted Motho Fela. They were glad to see him. Some had heard stories about him, but had never met him in person. He was also in a hurry to find out what the mood was like, and see how he could penetrate their secret conversations and hear what their fears and anxieties were. It didn't take much time to make progress.

Three hours into the shift the team leader, Albino Machel, opened up. They had just finished counting the gelatine sticks and checking the igniter gel in the explosives storage area.

Albino was well into his fifties. A foreigner, from Xai Xai in Mozambique, who had worked on the mine from the age of 19. Over the years he had taken many English lessons, because his Portuguese was not very helpful on the mine. Albino was not his real name. It was a nickname given to him by the men at the hostel, that emphasized the opposite of his extremely rich dark skin.

"You see Motho Fela, what the people want is fair treatment. We want fair compensation for the work we do. We are not planning to do anything stupid."

Motho Fela listened carefully, piecing together the puzzle. He decided to create an opportunity for his team leaders to meet with the other side, the officials. He would take them to the beer hall, near the main gate before driving home. He would stand up for multi-racialism, in a way that would allow his colleagues to start exploring their misgivings. He hoped to expose them to this new world, he had been part of for years now. Surprisingly, the hostel dwellers were excited to see their *umlungus* (officials). While some watched with suspicion, others came over and joined them. They laughed and spoke loudly, in case anyone observing from a distance suspected they were cooking up a nefarious plan.

5. 20/20 VISION

I See What They Can't See

In South Africa, a leader's visual acuity is measured by what they can see through the lens of race. Everything is about race. More so at work. That is what Kholofelo and Motho Fela had to contend with every day.

The looming strike at the mine was a prime example. It exposed what leaders on both sides of the racial divide could not see or understand about each other.

The arc of racial harmony bends at the leaders' ability to see beyond the haze that everyone is trapped in. The vision that guides the leader's decisions must be clear, regardless of the conditions; it must be articulated with definite purpose.

Motho Fela's vision was clear, and unconditioned. Young as he was, he already possessed rare qualities. You do not have to be a certain age to be a leader. Motho Fela was only 25, when he was thrown into the deep. He was clear that he was no one's puppet. The strings could not hold, because the identity he was making for himself had freed him from the puppet masters.

His resolve frightened those trapped in narrow social behaviour. He stood out amongst the rest of the graduates on the mine. At least that is how they thought of him at head office's graduate's journey mapping department. There was already talk about which graduates would make the fast-track leadership development programme. His name was on the list of those to be deployed to the new project at Kitwe in Zambia or at Maragoro in Tanzania.

He had no knowledge of the list drawn up by mnr Koekemoer along with officials from the training department on the graduate interview panel the previous December. He had impressed the panel, and had scored high on the candidate rating sheet. Besides the general questions that tested technical competency, knowledge,experience and personal attributes, there was one particular question that Motho Fela answered that convinced them he had the right stuff. It was a question on cross-cultural communication and racial co-operation. The question was, "How would you manage race and transformation issues on your production team, and maintain good morale?" The question aimed to gauge sensitivity to cultural diversity; facilitation of open exchange of ideas; building effective teamwork and cooperation. He thought for several seconds before answering with poise and confidence. "In my view, the story of the mine, is the story of South Africa. What happens at country level, filters down to us here on the mine. We cannot isolate ourselves from the winds of change. We are a microcosm of South Africa Incorporated. How we handle labour issues and stakeholder relations, must show that we recognise people as fellow human beings first and as workers and colleagues second. Our production targets rise and fall with our ability to track the happiness index. We must know one another. I would strive to be a present, visible and servant leader. I want to lead with humility. I must be alive to their needs, which means I must be there with them, at their level, where we can sweat it out together. That will help me build trust. It will open up multiple channels of free flowing communication and conflict resolution."

Motho Fela's level of clarity on the issues they tested him on, like business acumen; strategic thinking; project and risk management, was above average. The panel picked up that he was not the everyday type of mine personnel. His worldview was more liberated. In their discussions, they brushed it off as Jo'burg contamination that the mining system would soon flush out. Their observations on his outlook did not help them predict how he would handle things. The leadership approach at the mine in those days was still authoritarian drawing its inspiration from military discipline and rugby culture.

The winds of change that Motho Fela had referred to, had not yet blown over into the mining world. He was aware of that, and had told himself that he would use a more progressive range of leadership tools.

He would focus on making strong connections with both labourers and management; and lifting the veil on race issues so that he could rise above the quagmire.

Spaghetti Junction

One day after Motho Fela had spent time at the hostel, Spaghetti, the more seasoned shift boss in his section came over to ask him when he was going to the hostel again. He said he wanted to join their group. It would allow him, he said, to have eyes and ears on what was really going on; to win over some hearts.

Motho Fela knew there was no way to handle the task on his own. Like minded officials had to join in, bringing with them strengths and abilities he did not have. One gap was his lack of experience on the mine. He could benefit from the insights of his colleagues as well as their connections all the way to the top of the mine. He realised this early on.

When he got to the single quarters that afternoon, and had a chance to chat with the guys, he was able to gather intelligence. It turned out that even though the reasons for the strike were valid, it was also aimed at undermining the efforts of a new consultant head office had appointed to help them deal with declining production, a labour force that was increasingly unionised, and officials who were resisting transformation.

Motho Fela learned that the consultant was a controversial ex-mine official, who had taken early retirement, only to resurrect himself. He was well known throughout the mine. He had a reputation for siphoning off information and passing it on. Once the slanderous details reached the powers that be, you would be hit by a brick to the face, with no idea how they knew your thinking in the first place. This earned the consultant the nickname *Die Slang* (the snake). They said he had a forked tongue and that his venom spread slowly, silently shutting down your vital organs. "Once he's done with you, no one on the mine will dare come near you. You'll be treated like a leper. He will discredit you. Strip you of your dignity. Get people to treat you with suspicion. Eventually, you would lose your job or fire yourself"

After the conversation, Motho Fela showered and went for supper at *Madipere's Canteen.* That evening they had *bobotie* a Cape Dutch dish that consists of spiced mince, an egg-based topping with raisins, spiced with turmeric and curry. For desert he had *malva pudding* served with custard and vanilla ice cream. This is a single quarters guys' favourite.

After supper, he took a walk down to 23 Chesterton Rd, the commune where Kholofelo stayed. As usual, she was not watching television in the common room like the other girls. She was in her room, reading. The people around her had grown cold, jealous and judgemental, which pushed her to be even more bookish. Her best times were the moments she spent alone snuggled up in her room, reading. It gave her a chance to get lost in a world of stories, where life made sense and characters learned life lessons through adversity. She longed for the day where the challenges she faced would start making sense. Such was the state of mind Motho Fela found her in when he threw the door open, saying "Look who's here!"

Motho Fela's intention was to start mapping out his game plan. For that to happen, they first had to understand the feedback loops that had formed, which helped them to gain a clear perspective on things. They had to get to grips with the sequence of events, looking not only at what happened when, but at the how and possibly why. Operating in a dynamic and constantly evolving system takes your thinking to another level. Life in general comes packaged in a series of causes and effects. That is the essence of it all.

This skill Motho Fela was learning very rapidly – the ability to decipher how things influence each other in a system. His lessons about causality, made Kholofelo like him even more. Their relationship was proving fruitful and worth investing in. He was skilled at seeing the parts of a system and how they connect. With that information he could devise concrete plans on for dealing with the strike.

"And now that Spaghetti has joined us, things are going to be more exciting. You know baby, I am not going to be the odd one out anymore. There will be more voices singing from the same hymn sheet ..." and just before he could finish, Kholofelo burst out laughing because she just could not contain herself.

All these names that Motho Fela kept referring to were hilarious. It seemed like everyone at the mine had a nickname. "So wait baby why is this guy called Spaghetti, is he Italian?"

Motho Fela laughed back: "yeah the guy is of Italian origin. His real name is Mario Esposito. You know how guys at the mine can be. They didn't see themselves learning his complicated Italian name, so they called him Spaghetti because he is tall and has thin legs."

Kholofelo carried on laughing: "So are your guys aware that when Mario joins your exposition, they will have to start treating him with a bit of respect?"

If You Don't Play Politics, Politics Will Play You

There were a lot of moving parts in the mining leadership machine. Mining houses were mired in contrasting conditions. At national level there was a fresh focus on mining safety; environmental control and ownership of the mines. At the operations level there were more pressing matters to be handled. The unbundling of companies that used to be conglomerates had lifted a blanket that used to protect them against the hard socio-economic issues in the areas around the mines.

87% of mining labour was unionised. The wage bill was at its highest ever. Overstaffing was the big elephant in the room. The productivity-to-wage ratio was untenable. Frustrated senior managers on the mine would say "why can't we just get rid of surplus labour like data suggests?"

The townships around the mines were swelling with youngsters who had finished school in the rural areas and had moved in with relatives to look for jobs. This distorted regional unemployment figures. Some were squatting in the men's hostels, which increased water and electricity demand. Loitering was the order of the day. With so many idle souls roaming around, social instability and chaos emerged.

The local municipality suffered a devastating spill over effect. Refuse removal became unbearable. Dumping sites mushroomed everywhere. The infrastructure could not cater to all the demands. With rising unemployment fewer people were able to pay for services, leading to a new culture of non-payment and illegal electrical connections.

Relations between politicians and mine bosses were tested beyond measure. As relationships soured, service delivery was impacted. Mines use a lot of water. Deals between the municipality and the neighbouring farms had to be reviewed. As if that was not enough, there was also a rise in illegal mining.

The issuing of mining licenses had come under the spotlight, and the Mining Charter review process was taking long. Local police had too much on their hands. There were fatalities reported daily at the illegal mining operations. Arrests had to be made at the mine because retrenched mine workers were colluding with mining officials who let them onto the mine with fake clock cards.

"Gentlemen," said Mnr Koekemoer as he concluded his planning meeting with the shift bosses and mine captains, "we are dealing here with a labour union led by people who use jargon like 'neoliberal agenda' and 'exploitation of the proletariat'. Clearly they have no place on the mine; they don't have our interests at heart. They spend more time studying outdated political philosophy than modern mining economics. This is a mine. We produce gold here. Nothing else."

No one said anything; not because they agreed with his view of the situation, but because they respected his position as production manager.

Some saw union organizers as parasites they could not get rid of. Others described them as "…children who refuse to grow up, who never wash their dishes or clean up after themselves; children who eat all the food in the fridge, no matter how much you stock it up. When you come home from work, you find them loafing around. They don't make up their beds, but they're the first ones to complain about the menu, and demand that their allowances be increased."

No Such Thing as Perfect Vision

This was the reality that recent graduates like Motho Fela had to learn, and learn fast. The bargaining power of unions was unprecedented. Over the years, unions had strengthened their ranks with educated, sophisticated negotiators.

In their scenario planning, the mining houses had not invested much in how to deal with this new threat. Leadership, predominantly university graduates, were highly skilled in mining engineering, but were clueless when it came to dealing with shaft stewards and *toyi-toyi* dancing, machete wielding protestors.

Universities were churning out youngsters who could not read the highly volatile social and socio-economic dynamics. South Africa was fast becoming the industrial protest capital of the world. Organisations were under pressure to respond to protests effectively, not as victims but as victors.

Few leaders are able to see everything going on. Your visual range as a leader is limited. You need others; you cannot do it alone.

The idea of 20/20 vision is based on the Snellen Fractions, a measurement system developed by Dutch ophthalmologist Dr Herman Snellen in 1862. His famous eye chart tests you from a viewing distance of 20 feet, or 6 metres. The letters on the chart differ in size using standardized line separating the big from the small letters.

If you have no problem seeing the letters placed along that line, but are struggling to see anything smaller, you are considered to have normal vision or '20/20 visual acuity'.

The numerator on the Snellen Fraction is your distance away from the eye chart. The denominator is the size of letters you are able to see on the chart.

If, for instance, your results are 20/40 vision, then it means you are able to see big letters from the number 40 line and above. If your results are 20/10, then it means you are able to see big letters and small letters down to the number 10 line, and your vision is better than 20/20. If your score is 20/200, you are considered legally blind.

No leader wants to be classified legally blind, but unfortunately that's what one can say for those who refer to trade unionists as rabble rousers; or who practise creative accounting, bribery; job reservation; nepotism, discrimination, bullying and constructive dismissal. All of these are at the root of defined blindness and should be dealt with in all organizations without fear or favour.

The strain Motho Fela was feeling at work, started to show in his interactions at the single quarters and in his relationship with Kholofelo. He was irritable. At the slightest provocation, he would be agitated, enough so that others would notice. Few were brave enough to give him feedback. But Kholofelo wouldn't have any of it.

She snapped back at him one day at the movies in Klerksdorp. As they walked into Leba Movie Theatre, Kholofelo dropped popcorn all over the floor, to which Motho Fela said "Can't you see where you're walking, what's wrong with you?"

Kholofelo was livid: "Do you want a list? I can give it to you."

Conquering Self First

During the movie they were quiet. They never said a word to each other. Motho Fela was not too fond of the movies. It was Kholofelo's thing. He went along to be with her. Watching the movie gave them time to think, an opportunity to detach emotionally while sitting together physically.

They were both vulnerable. It exposed an aspect of their relationship they had thought they had risen above. But, all relationships have mountains and valleys. Both are necessary to strengthen them. Vulnerability deconstructs falsehood. It rearranges the facts before it puts everything back together in a new form.

"Of all the ways you could have spoken to me, was that the best you could think of? I will not have you speaking to me like that. That's not how we should talk to each other. You're taking things out on me. The pressure you're getting from Mnr Koekemoer to be his informant has nothing to do with me. I will not be your punching bag."

There was more quiet in the car, as they drove back to Orkney. Motho Fela put on some music, hoping it would set her soul on fire. When her mother thought she was old enough, she had introduced her to Nina Simone. Though it was not to Motho Fela's taste, for the sake of the relationship he played *Young Black and Gifted*.

Kholofelo had not seen it coming. It was so appropriate, it fitted her thoughts like a glove. The lyrics made her heart melt:

To be young, gifted and black
Oh what a lovely precious dream
To be young, gifted and black
Open your heart to what I mean
In the whole world you know
There are billion boys and girls
Who are young, gifted and black,
And that's a fact.
Young, gifted and black
We must begin to tell our young
There's a world waiting for you
This is a quest that's just begun.
When you feel really low

Soothing as the music was, she could not see his true intentions. Motho Fela had that rare skill of deep listening. He remembered the things Kholofelo spoke about passionately. He paid special attention to what touched her deep within. And he challenged his ego to get out of the way so that his vision could be clear. He faltered sometimes. He wasn't consistent. He was still learning the art. But Kholofelo appreciated the effort, how he waged the battle with himself. You can't win the battle with others until you've won the battle with yourself.

6. A LEADER'S EYE

Unprecedented Bold Moves

Mnr Koekemoer put together a negotiation team to face the union. He called the mine captain, and arranged the meeting through his sister, Claudette, for them to meet with the general manager, Mr Jacob Jannaway at his house after work. In that way they would find him relaxed enough to discuss tough issues. When they got there, he welcomed them with shots of 18 year old Glenfiddich. He wanted the whiskey to set the serious tone for this important matter.

"Gentlemen, thank you for arranging this. You know how much I value having you as my co-pilots at the east mine. You are my eyes and ears. I am counting on you. I trust you. We have fought serious battles together and won. We have to win this one as well. You were there in 1987 for that big strike that changed everything about how we handle industrial action. We don't want this situation to spiral into something like that. You know how much our lack of unity as mine officials, from head office all the way down to our level in operations, opened up space for the union to capitalise on. Negotiation is how we handle things now. No confrontation. That has been institutionalised officially. You know that. So I want us to come up with a clear plan for this negotiation process, and decide on who we are going to make part of our team."

That is when Mnr Koekemoer first thanked the GM for his visionary leadership and wise counsel, before he said *"Meneer* (sir) I think in our team we have to include all stakeholders. We have to first consult widely, within the mine fraternity but also ensure that we engage openly with the police and the Department of Labour. We might have to do a bit of homework on the Commission for Conciliation Mediation and Arbitration, to be clear on their procedures. But I have another important point to raise *meneer*. In our bid to be as inclusive as possible, I think we need to bring in people that would otherwise not be a part of something serious like this. I think we have to be bold, and bring in the bright young graduates we have at the shaft and also those who have worked in production for a long time."

The GM liked the sound of that, and asked him if he had anyone in mind. *"Ja Meneer*, there is this new guy from Wits University that seems to have formed strong relationships with the labourers in the hostel. His name is Gert du Toit. The men call him Motho Fela, sir. They love him. He even has a black girlfriend. We could use him as a bridge to connect us with these union people. And then I was thinking of this Italian fellow, Mario Esposito. He has been in my section for years now. He is doing very well. He hits production targets all the time. Last year he won the Chairman's Production Trophy. I am sure you remember him. He has a clear grasp of what gets the guys motivated. He would be a great asset for us"

He didn't need to explain any further, the GM was already sold. He loved the idea. Claudette brought in the supper. They spent the rest of the evening talking over the finer details, enjoying their wickedly, strong poison.

Early in the morning the following day, Motho Fela and Spaghetti were called into Mnr Koekemoer's office an hour before they went underground. When they shut the door behind them, Mnr Koekemoer pulled the blinds so that no passers-by could see what was going on. He told them he believed that battles are won in the general's tent. He told them that the GM wanted them to be involved in the negotiations. And, in that hour he wanted to hear their views on how the negotiations had to be handled, and what tactics they could use. Spaghetti had spent time with Motho Fela discussing ideas on the strike without knowing that they would come into good use. So, he spoke first: *"Meneer*, I think a lot of clues lie in our historical experiences. The last big strike we had in 1987 caused a lot of damage. Its implications were big for both the mine and the union. There are no winners in a strike. We have to find a way to prevent it. That strike went on for three weeks, if you remember. One production day lost, is one day too many. We can't afford that. The timing of the strike was wrong. Not that it can ever be right, but I am referring to what was happening in the country back then. Former President P. W. Botha's security forces in the townships were acting with a heavy hand, and were met with a lot of resistance. We don't want to put paraffin on the fire again. The ANC has a big conference in December. President Mandela might announce his retirement, and we don't know who will take over. There is instability in the country as it is. This would look like we are not learning anything from history."

Then Motho Fela spoke about the negotiation approach, focusing on what he called the five major points to keep in mind at the negotiation table. "We will only sign a wage deal with the union if we give them something that addresses more issues than they have presented to us. We need to talk about bigger issues, like dignity and respect. Top of that list is the question of housing. If we can present something about the company's medium term goals on housing, which includes doing away with single sex hostels, giving them the option to bring their families from the rural areas to where they work, that will gain us some negotiation muscle. Maybe one of the senior officials can table a deal that would span more than one year to three years into the future."

He then detailed the five main points, writing them on the flip chart in the corner:

1. Financial Reward System – what their financial proposal was, demonstrating affordability
2. Operational Management – discuss the impact on productivity, and the expenses thereof
3. Communication – create channels for frank, open and continuous communication
4. Training and Development – sweeten the deal with upskilling
5. Health and Safety – remind them about our efforts to improve the environment they work in

The following week on Wednesday, a settlement was reached. Both parties emerged from the negotiations extremely happy. They reported that the deal was fair and it addressed issues that would bring stability and dignity in the medium term.

Motho Fela was hailed as the hero of the process. He had impressed his superiors, and shown his worth as a future leader. The union bosses were happy that they had clinched a three year deal that guaranteed a R500 increase on monthly basic pay plus other benefits like ex-gratia payments of R1000 per employee at the end of the month and another R1000 in December before Christmas.

In this way the strike was averted. The name that was on everyone's lips at the mine was Motho Fela. They would ask themselves, *"Ke mang Motho Fela* (Who is Motho Fela)?" and the answer would always be *"Ke motho fela* (He is just a fellow human being)."

One Tear One Smile

The letter from head office came, eventually, confirming that Motho Fela, together with two other graduates, had been selected for placement in the Zambian Copper Belt, for a period of twelve months. They had picked one graduate per department on merit.

Motho Fela was an obvious choice from mining operations because of his sterling work in averting the strike, which could have cost the mine millions. In metallurgy they chose Anushka Pillay for her successful project at the smelter. In engineering they thought Khathu Ramasha would be a valuable resource for the vibration analysis research he had done on Ball Mills. There was no one from geology and rock mechanics, or from the survey, safety and environmental departments.

Excited, Motho Fela took the afternoon off, and informed his mine captain but not Mnr Koekemoer that he had made it into the top three for Zambia. He could not wait to tell Kholofelo the great news. He didn't know who else would be joining him in Zambia. He prayed that the big wigs at head office had done the right thing, and included the love of his life on that list. He could not imagine life without her for a full year, let alone the fact that it would be in a foreign country. He was acquainted with other graduates from all departments, especially those who had studied at Wits. Those who came from the University of Pretoria or University of Cape Town were still strangers to him. Even though they had attended a few short courses on the mine together, they had not formed any real connections.

On his way from the shaft to Orkney, he kept calling Kholofelo on her cell phone. There was no response. It just kept ringing. He didn't want to leave a voice mail. That would spoil everything. Then he remembered that she might still be underground because on Thursdays they spent more time underground 'licking rocks', as Motho Fela would often tease her. After trying twice, he decided to call her for the last time and if she didn't answer he would just leave a voice message.

"Hey baby, I have been trying to get hold of you all day. I wanted to let you know that I took the afternoon off. When you get this message, I will either be at the single quarters or at the rec club. Call me."

By the time he got to Orkney there was still no response. He went to his place. But then realised how dead it was, with everyone still at work. He could either sleep for a few hours, so that he could party all night or just go to the rec club for the rest of the afternoon. He knew that at least there he would find some company.

He walked in and went straight to the bar area. He ordered a gin and tonic. The waiter put it in front of him, with two little bowls. One had chilly bites of game biltong, the other had peanuts. When he took the first sip, he felt someone patting him on his back. He turned around to see that it was Kenny, a night time shift boss from his section. He was on the same programme with him. Motho Fela didn't know what his outcome had been. So he was not so sure what to say. He had to think fast, and be clear which details he would share and which to keep to himself.

"Congratulations man! I heard you made it into the top three for Zambia. You deserve it my brother. *Shaya la* (put it here)."

After a high five and a low five, Kenny told him what was on his mind. "I understand that this is head office's way of rewarding you for stopping the strike. But to be honest, my view is they could have given you recognition in another way. As for the Accelerated Leadership Development Programme, I think they made a mistake selecting a white candidate. Who really needs affirmative action in this country? It's us, not you. We are more deserving of fast-track programmes so that we can start taking up the positions that used to be reserved for you guys..."

While Kenny was venting, another guy walked in and joined them at the bar. It was Pottie, the hefty gentle giant. Pottie Potgieter was a rugby player, on the mine's first team, who was also a member of the mine proto team. Putting out fires was his thing. He worked only on call outs, whenever there was an emergency like methane gas explosions or people trapped underground, he would be part of the emergency rescue team.

"You know I could hear you Kenny from right there", Pottie said, pointing to the far end of the rec club where he had been finishing his beer. "Come on man, why don't you just admit it? *Jy is jaloers* (You are jealous). It has nothing to do with politics. Your chance will come one day. Relax."

This annoyed Kenny, but before he could respond, Motho Fela asked a quick question. "Wait wait Kenny, how did you find out?" Kenny then explained that one of the benefits of working night shift is that you are the first to get the latest news on the mine. He heard it through the grapevine. The head of training, Peter Patterson's son, who also worked night shift but in another section, had shared the news with at the change house the previous night. This piece of information was important for Motho Fela.

The conversation carried on, and Kenny was a bit calmer, because Pottie offered to buy them the next round. Motho Fela stepped a few metres away from them and the noise from the sound speakers on the walls, to take a call on his cell phone. It was Kholofela. She wanted to tell him that she was still at the mine and had received his message. Then he told her that she had to drive straight to the rec club, but did not explain why.

Two and a half hours later when she finally arrived, Pottie and Kennny were still there. They were in high spirits, and a bit loud. Before she could greet them, Kenny stood up with a glass in his hand and said, "Okay go on, you can give your man a big kiss on the lips. It might be your last one. He's off to Zambia next month. From now on you will be stuck with the likes of me." He staggered over to her, with a lewd look in his eyes.

"Baby what's he talking about? said Kholofelo. Motho Fela, already standing up, opened his arms and gave her a kiss on the forehead and hugged her passionately. Pottie and Kenny looked on: one with admiration, the other with envy. This was a private moment she would rather have shared at his place. But there it was.

When everyone was calm and the jealousy issues had been dealt with politely, thanks to Pottie's diplomacy, it was time for Kholofelo to share her news.

"I have also been selected, for Tanzania. I will go to Maragoro for a year. Me and two other graduates will join the exploration team, starting next month."

This was a double whammy for Motho Fela. On one hand it was exciting. He had to show how happy he was for her. On another hand, what might it do to their relationship? Decisions had been made, there was no turning back. All that was left was for them to start sorting out passports and visas.

On hearing this, a cold tear dropped from Motho Fela's eye. He was trying to put on a brave face. It was going to be their first time away from each other for such a long time.

Pottie loved watching the fireworks. For Kenny, it was not great news. Just when he thought the *mlungu* (white) boyfriend would be out of the way so that he could try his luck with Kholofelo! What a slap to the face.

A Room with a Light

Towards the beginning of July, winter at its peak, the time came for them to pack their bags and say goodbye to the world of *Madipere, Spaghetti, Albino* and Mnr Koekemoer. A big send-off party was organised for all the graduates who were leaving. It was hosted by the GM at Vaal River Lagoon, an exclusive venue used only on prestigious occasions. All the important people were there – the head of training, mr. Peter Patterson and all the heads of department. Even Mnr Koekermoer was there, as Motho Fela's *makhulu baas* (big boss).

After the host had made his welcome speech, he handed over to the head of training to give the keynote address, sharing the critical information they had to keep in mind and how much the company was investing in them. Halfway through his speech he explained the Accelerated Leadership Development Programme.

> "….The company has partnered with one of the top business schools in the country, GIBS (the Gordon Institute of Business Leadership). This Accelerated Leadership Development Programme is a three year programme. Today marks the beginning of the first year. Nine of you have been selected, out of the total 21 graduates we have on the mine. After careful consideration, from the outcomes of the psychometrics and your performance these six months on the mine, we have concluded that you will be on the first cohort to pilot this programme. You are our guinea pigs. We have all the confidence in you. We are placing you in three different regions in Africa where the company already has business interests. Who knows, maybe when you've finished, those are the operations you will end up being managers in. In each region we are placing three of you. For east Africa, we are sending you to Maragoro in Tanzania, at the Mapenzi Mining & Exploration Company. For West Africa, we are taking you to Sadiola in Mali, hope you guys will come back fluent in French. And for central southern Africa three of you will be working at Kitwe on Zambia's Copper Belt. The future

leaders of our business have to have intimate knowledge of doing business on the continent. Gone are the days where we used to think that only Europe and America could offer superior learning experiences. After a year you will then come back to Johannesburg, for block release studies at GIBS. You will be accommodated at the apartment block above the Rand Club in Marshalltown, which is a stone's throw away from head office. You will carry on with your work on the mine and get exposure to different leadership roles. While you are away, you will be given three weeks leave to visit home or to explore your host country. We will continue paying the same salary you are getting now."

The rest of the evening went well, and everyone behaved themselves until the big bosses left. Then they hit the bar. The drinking spree went on until just after midnight. The following day, they all assembled at Number One training centre.

Victor then drove them off to the Johannesburg International Airport in the mine's 27 seater bus. Along the way they were singing and taking pictures. Excitement was in the air.

Anxiety was also evident. For most it was positive anticipation, but with some of them had heard horror stories about the rest of Africa.

As for Kholofelo and Motho Fela the only thing on their minds was about how they were going to keep the fires burning while they are going to be living in different countries. The only consolation was that Kitwe is only a two hour flight away from Tanzania.

They arrived at the airport, and headed straight to their respective check-in counters. They were all flying South African Airways. The six heading for east and west Africa were on SAA F202 to Nairobi in Kenya, where after a 45 minute layover they would connect to Dar es Salaam in Tanzania and Bamako in Mali. Motho Fela, Khathu and Anushka had it easy. They only had one flight to catch, no layovers no connections. They were flying SAA F731 to Ndola, where an official from Kita-Kita Copper Mine was going to take them to their new home in Kitwe. At the international departures lounge, they did not have much time to say their goodbyes. As soon as they were done with customs flight SAA F731 was called up, and a teary Motho Fela had to grab his bags and run.

Luckily he sat near the window and the two seats next to him were empty. Khathu was also alone, two rows behind Motho Fela. Anushka sat on a three seater, which he shared with an old man that looked like he was soon going to be snoring, so she moved over to an empty three seater row.

After take-off, with turbulence gone, he greeted the two people sitting on the other side of the aisle. They asked him where he was going. He shared the details, saying how lucky he was to have been chosen, and how excited he was to be flying out of South Africa for the first time. He told them about the sacrifices in his personal life; the give and take he had to deal with. They could not relate, because they were living in a different world.

When the plane landed two hours later in Ndola he found himself witnessing a surprise show. As they stepped out of the aircraft to descend the stairs, he noticed a contingent of journalists and photographers, and women gyrating their hips in unison, singing traditional songs. The women in front were carrying colourful garlands. As Motho Fela and his fellow graduates got close, the singing got louder and the women came closer. They came straight towards them, and knelt on the ground, before them. He heard words like 'halleluyah' and 'hosanna' in a strange dialect. Motho Fela did not know what was going on. The cameras were clicking away, and the flashlights had a dizzying effect.

Then two men placed their hands on the heads of the singing ladies who kneeled to pray. A few minutes later the ladies stood up, and placed the garlands over the shoulders of the graduates.

Then a big man, who looked like an American rapper because of the gold chains and basketball sneakers he was wearing stepped forward and said, "Ladies, the flowers are not for them. They are meant for me, Prophet Surprise Nyemba and my friend Pastor Ray Merkel over here. You can take the flowers off their shoulders. Sorry guys". The ladies did as they were told. Only then did Motho

Fela realise he had been in the company of two local celebrity church leaders.

As soon as they were done with the customs procedures, they stepped outside the small building and saw a friendly faced middle-aged man carrying a placard with their names on it. It was their driver, Nevermind, who looked as if he had been waiting for them in the scorching sun for a few hours.

They greeted him. Khathu, trying to outshine them, said hello in *Bemba*, the dominant language in the area. The thirty minute drive out of Ndola, via the stadium went by quickly. They got to Chililongo Guest House in no time.

When Anushka had checked and was out of sight, Nomatter, the Receptionist asked Motho Fela and Khathu if they wanted a room with light or not. They looked at each other, and didn't understand what she meant. "Obviously our rooms have to have lights. Is that something we have to make special arrangements for?" Then she gave them the keys, and because the guest house was not that big, it was easy for them to find their way around following the markings on the walls.

The first thing Motho Fela did when he got to the room was drop his bags, and head straight for the shower. He wanted to wash off the dust and stickiness brought on by the humid July air.

Then came a knock on the door. He turned off the shower and asked "Who is it?" A female voice replied "It's me, Sharon. I am the light, you asked for'.

Zambia on My Mind

Back at Johannesburg International Airport there was drama. The graduates connecting from Nairobi to Dar es Salaam heard an announcement that their flight had been delayed. There was a maintenance issue.

A rumour started spreading through the lounge that the real reason for the delay was that smoke had been detected near the aircraft's engine compartment.

Then, a second announcement: Repairs would take longer than expected. They would now fly Kenya Airways instead and would be accommodated at a Mombasa hotel overnight. The following morning they would take a connecting flight to neighbouring Tanzania. Apologies.

Half an hour later they were on their way.

Kholofelo nodded off. She woke up to the voice of a flight steward, making the landing announcement. The plane descended into the breath taking, early evening, city lights of Nairobi, hugging what Kholofelo thought was Mount Kenya. The plane landed and as they taxied to the terminal building a voice over the intercom said *"Mabibi namabuwana, karibuni* Jomo Kenyatta International Airport. Ladies and Gentlemen, welcome to Jomo Kenyatta International Airport."

All of a sudden, hearing passengers speaking *KiSwahili* all around her, it dawned on her that she was far from home; a new chapter in her life was about to unfold.

Soon they were on a bus to Mombasa. Surprisingly it was full of passengers. Only a few seats were open. It turned out to be a commuter bus carrying people home from work in the city. It had been detoured to the airport to pick up the stranded travellers. They squeezed in and made themselves comfortable. It was a bumpy ride. The road was filled with pot holes.

Kholofelo sat next to a chatty old lady, only too happy to explain what she should expect in Kenya. "If you look out the window and you see two shiny eyes, just know it could be a giraffe stuck in a pot hole." They laughed and Kholofelo relaxed. Then the old lady jumped up and got off at the Indian-owned Mariketi Bazaar.

They arrived at the hotel about ninety minutes later. By then it was after 22h00. It was a dilapidated place, whose lobby showed features of its glorious colonial past.

The music playing was Ray Charles' *Georgia on My Mind*. Kholofelo found herself singing along, but replacing the word *Georgia* with *Zambia*.

She was not bothered by the slow check-in process. She leaned over the counter, staring through the window, into the moonlight. Swaying to the gentle rhythm, she could see herself in the arms of Motho Fela.

Second Moment to Pause

1. What is the state of your psychological shock absorbers?
2. What personal strengths and qualities do you intentionally bring in to your work experience?
3. How are you contributing towards the dismantling of toxicity in your organization?
4. What is it that you can see, but have noticed that those around you can't see?
5. What bridges are you building, for yourself and others, to cross the racial-divide?
6. How are you keeping your fingers on the pulse, and always in touch with reality?
7. In which way are you taking up space, and shaking things up?
8. When driving a strategic agenda, what leadership approach works best for you?
9. In your actions and efforts, how do you balance structure with flexibility?
10. How do you ensure that your ego does not trip you over, as you plan your moves?

SECTION 3: MIRROR (THE PRESENT)

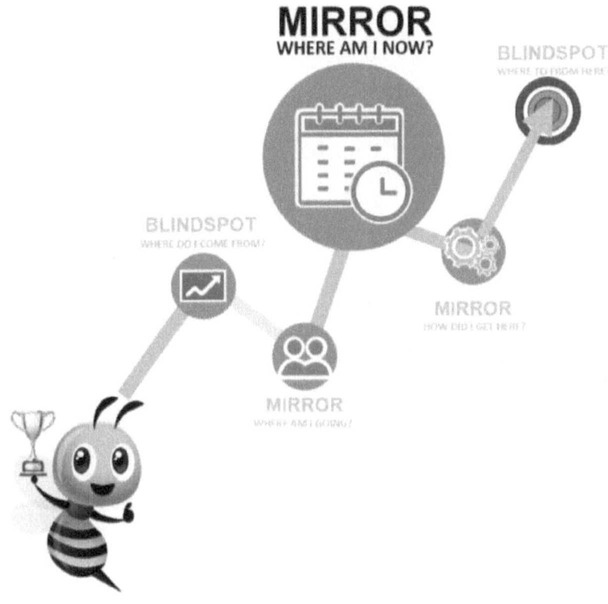

"But any time is with us. And if we take control to shape our attitude and reshape our memories, that time is always now - our time for the best possible uses of our lives." - **Keorapetse Kgositsile**

7. VISUAL RANGE

Surprise Benefits of International Exposure

Word on the streets and corridors at the mine, after the year 2000 Accelerated Leadership Development Program cohort had left, was "What if they train them for three years, and they leave?" And to that some would respond by saying, "What if they don't train them, and they stay?"

There were no guarantees for the company. Not even the contract they had signed with the nine delegates was proof that they would return and plough back what they had learned in the programme. People movement is something unpredictable. With freedom, comes a wide range of choices that people can make. No one can control that. For a person who is scared of venturing into the unknown that could be a scary idea, but for the free adventurous soul freedom could be similar to a blank canvass where one can stroke the brush in any direction they want.

All three groups settled well in their host countries. There were not so many issues to contend with. The new colleagues they had been introduced to were excited to have them in their midst, hoping to learn as much about South African culture as possible; in return, promising that they would expose them to as much of their own culture, both in the workplace and outside of work. It was only the West African trio that complained, in their email communication, about intermittent power failure. They shared stories about how electricity in the region was sourced from a big power station in Nigeria, and supplied all the countries in that region. That was through bilateral power deals facilitated by the respective governments and the Nigerian Electricity Power Authority, NEPA, which people referred to as *Never Expect Power Always* because of its unreliability.

Kholofelo and her buddies in the land of uJaamah and uMoja, were already learning KiSwahili and were immersed deeply in the progressive cultural dynamics of life in East Africa. The contrasts between the East and the West were huge. They spoke of how vast the continent is, and how in that expanse of land, also lay the ruins of a painful colonial past. The language differences; the religious divide and the horrible emotional scars that were evident in people's faces everywhere they went. In West Africa, the three young uninitiated academics came face to face with the harsh realities of how the colonial corruption of minds and souls, in the pursuit of an ignoble effort to perpetrate a veritable crime against humanity, had dehumanised both the oppressors and the oppressed. Their close proximity to Timbuktu in Mali gave them access to a proud African Arabic heritage that they knew nothing about; from the red clay architecture to goat herding and to the Islamic religion itself. They were blown away by the richness, depth and fusion of the Arabic, Fulani, Bambara and Tuareg cultures. On weekends they would visit the great historical sites and mosques such as the Djinguereber, Sankore and the Sidi Yahia, which are attributed to the founders of the nation such as Emperor Mansa Musa. They learned about how trade had been hard-wired into the hearts and minds of people in West Africa many centuries ago, through the salt and gold trade.

In the copper capital of the world, Motho Fela would spend most of his evenings at the large balcony of his room with Khathu and Anushka. Their conversations would vary from the impressive work ethic they witnessed at the mine, to abject poverty that dominated all the areas the copper mines were operating from. It just did not make sense to them. They would ask themselves 'how could it be that such a rich area, that lies on the major trade route between the Democratic Republic of Congo and Botswana and South Africa on the far south, could have so much wealth and yet none of it was accessible to the local people?" They spoke about the prostitutes who would have to sell their bodies and souls to long distance cross-border Truck Drivers to assuage hunger. They contrasted it with the same realities back home in South Africa.

As time went by, a new level of awareness started creeping in. They became more in touch with who they were as individuals.

They started questioning their attitudes towards the continent, and found themselves having to overhaul their beliefs and fears. They started accepting that they were a part of Africa. It didn't matter what the colour of their skin was. They were all Africans. The transitional state of being that this experience had thrown them into, was a rude awakening. Motho Fela went as far as keeping the camera, that he used to carry with him everywhere he went, in the safe at the guest house. He had no more use for it. He thought he had to turn the lens on himself. It was on himself, and fellow white South Africans back home, that he needed to do some examining. Not the innocent souls in Kitwe.

When people visit countries like the United States, they don't go around taking random pictures of children playing in the streets, but when they visit Africa, they do. That is the level of thoughtfulness that Motho Fela had grown into, in the six months that he had spent in Zambia. While he was excited about the upcoming three weeks leave that coincided with the Christmas holidays, he was also anxious about whether his tourist visa application to visit Kholofelo in Tanzania would be processed in time. He wanted to spend the entire three weeks with her, and had a huge surprise up his sleeve. They communicated daily via email, and spoke on the phone once a week, because of the exorbitant hotel costs on international calls.

All of them, in their different host countries were registering serious progress. As part of the programme they had to work in all departments on the mine. It didn't matter what their qualification was. They would spend three weeks in Employee Relations, and learn about human resource matters; from there they would move on to Finance and Accounts, where they would learn about mining economics, finance and deal making and so on. By the time the twelve months were over, they would have a big picture view and a clear understanding of what a typical mining operation is structured. This would give them hands-on knowledge and appreciation of all the parts of the value chain. They would come out with real skills in project management; leadership and conflict resolution.

The programme was designed in such a way that when they were due to start the second leg of their programme at GIBS, then they would be taught through action-learning. This would help them develop personal power techniques, and be able to convert appropriate theory learned in the class-room into practical application at the mine. That process would further help them shape their leadership styles and behaviours. They had already begun working on their personal development plans, and they were all making remarkable progress in that regard.

In their weekly email communication, they talked about how happy and stress free they were. They were treated like royalty at the mines. People celebrated them everywhere. They were tourists, and culture samplers of note. Zambia, because of its geographical disposition, gave Motho Fela, Khathu and Anushka a chance to taste a bit of Zimbabwe; DRC; Angola; Botswana and Malawi. Their visa's allowed them as South Africans to cross the borders as long as they proved that they were going to come back into Zambia within permissible stay periods. The most remarkable experience was when they organised a road trip with Nevermind, to Livingstone where they could cross over the Zambezi River into Victoria Falls. They paid the US$20 dollar tourist fee for them to spend a day in there. They saw the David Livingstone statue, and spent quality time in front of the 108m drop of water, witnessing the famous water thunder and smoke. They were elevated to a uniquely spiritual feel to find themselves in the spot which David Livingstone on the 16th of November 1855 had stood. That was the place where him and his Makololo assistants had looked down into the seething cauldron beneath them, getting drenched in the mist, where they could see rainbows in the horizon. That was the angelic place that had inspired him to record in his journal everything that had happened as he lay on his stomach on the lip of the falls saying that:

"On the left side of the island we have a good view of the water, as it leaps quite clear of the rock, and forms a thick unbroken fleece all the way to the bottom. Its whiteness gave the idea of snow, a sight I had not seen for many a day" and concluded that it was "the most wonderful sight" he had seen in Africa.

The Interpretation of the African Dream

When Motho Fela walked into the Chililongo Guest House, after work on the 1st of December, Nomatter stopped him and told him that there was a thick brown formal envelope for him to sign off. It was a letter and his passport from the Travel Agent in Lusaka. It had his Tanzanian visa already suffixed to page 3 of his passport. He was so relieved. Immediately he asked Nomatter to dial up the number at Kholofelo's hotel in Maragoro.

"Baby guess what I am carrying in my hands right now" and she knew exactly what he was excited about. They spoke about the major details of his visit and started exploring ways in which they could spice things up. He did not reveal much. After finalizing all travel arrangements, off he went. And they were united again, after such a long time away from each other. The social distance was too much for them, and they had to keep the fires burning.

They checked into Kipepeo Beach Hotel in Dar es Salaam, and stayed only for one night. The following day Motho Fela, early in the morning, stepped outside, and disappeared for a good three hours. He never told Kholofelo where he was going. This was unusual. She had no reason to worry, because after all they were in the home of peace. This former German East African city was the mecca of African fashion, art, music, film and fancy jewellery. She thought Motho Fela might have wondered off into the flea markets, and would most probably be bringing her great mementos.

Just after 9AM he returned back to the hotel, and found Kholofelo ready for breakfast downstairs, for which they were only left with one hour to rush to. When they finished with breakfast, instead of going back to their room there was a *tuk-tuk* waiting for them outside. It was draped in beautiful colourful petals all over. Motho Fela was surprisingly quiet for a lovely morning like that. The driver seemed to be in on the details where all that was leading to.

After five minutes they found themselves at the north side of the White Sands Beach, where a dow was waiting for them. It ferried them across to the secluded island, away from the hustle and bustle of the busy economically vibrant city of Dar. It was like they were in paradise. Its long stretches of sandy beach tranquillity only had two guys roaming around aimlessly. Its shores were lapped by warm, calm ocean water. When they got off the dow, and took off their flip-flops to walk barefoot, the two guys on the beach then turned around towards them, and whisked out big white boards with words "MARRY" "ME" on them. By the time Kholofelo saw them do that, she turned around and found Motho Fela on his knees with a diamond ring in his hands. "Yes Yes Yes Yes Yes", those were the only words she managed to get out of her mouth. They embraced passionately and cried together.

The two guys then led them to the island underground walk-in glass aquarium, where they could take a stroll viewing all sorts of fish and sea life directly in its natural form. They came out of there still joined at the hip. They took a long walk exploring the tiny island together, hand in hand and chick to chick. Around lunch time they walked into the weekend island. They were served ndizi-nyama, which was generous portions of plantains with meat that Kholofelo wanted Motho Fela to taste. She was fluent in KiSwahili by then. She read the menu with ease and speak to the locals without any difficulty. KiSwahili is very similar to the Nguni variety of languages from back home in South Africa. It only differs where it infuses Arabic and Indian influences on the language. While Motho Fela was still feasting at the table, she went over to the main counter, asked for the Manager.

"Nitumie simu tafadhali" (May I use the phone please)

She wanted to call her mother and tell her the good news, and ask her not to tell anyone. It was going to be a quick call, so that she could only pay the restaurant only Five Thousand Tanzanian Shillings, which is about R40 in South Africa.

The three weeks went very quick for them, and before Motho Fela could pack his bags and head back to Zambia, it was already New

Year. They celebrated the dawn of a new era in Zanzibar, on one of their romantic excursions. While on the island they kept contact with family back home. They also made a point of phoning some of their mates back at the mine in Orkney, just to check how they were doing.

A big turn off for Motho Fela, when talking to people back in South Africa, was to hear how stuck up they were. He felt they were cocooned in lofty enclaves of privilege and supremacy. If he had things his own way, he would make it a rule that all South Africans would be issued with an Identity Document and a Passport right as soon as they started school, so that they could travel and see what else was out there in the world. His exposure into the continent, opened his eyes to see the large scale of how much Africans had been given the bum end of the stick. He really felt there was a need for a national project for the whole country to rethink the questions of race, identity and responsibility.

Multiplicity and Overlap of Systems

The year 2000 started on a high note for Motho Fela and Kholofelo. They were familiar with how things worked at their host countries. They knew how to mix and mingle. They had made new friends, and formed strong networks with other ambitious youngsters they found there. As for Motho Fela, he had made connections with the Chinese expats who were working at Kita-Kita Mine. They talked about a lot of great opportunities, not only in Asia but in the rest of the world. Their world view was much broader than his. They considered themselves as citizens of the world. Their lives were not limited to China, but were open to live and work anywhere in the world.

That made him to start getting really curious about Asia. He started doing a bit of research about the different countries there. He was particularly attracted to Thailand in South East Asia. He loved how progressive Thai people were, in terms of culture and religion. He went on and started doing a lot of digging up about the country and what it has to offer in terms of study opportunities, more especially on something that he knew could not be found in South Africa.

At the end of June, they finished their programme in the continent and it was time to go back home. When they arrived at the mine, they were welcomed back with a huge party, bigger than the time they left the previous year. This time around their parents had come over, from all across the country to be a part of the festivities. It was like a huge graduation party. In the audience were also Professors from the University of Pretoria who taught at GIBS.

Kholofelo's mom noticed something strange with her. She had a bun in the oven. Her father did not see anything, because of her big overcoat, she kept on for the winter cold weather. He only noticed that her face was chubby, and thought that maybe it was because she had been well taken care of by the people of Mwalimu Julius Nyerere.

The programme had been modified a little. Their first six months back in South Africa were going to be spent at the mine doing experiential learning. This involved taking up junior management positions, or acting on behalf of any of their superiors who wanted to take leave. It was a vigorous program, that allowed them to introduce all the exciting stuff they had learned in the continent. Motho Fela and his Zambian buddies had been exposed to massive mining operation and productivity. Kita-Kita Mine was producing 300 000 tons of copper each year, through the process of open stoping. They learned a lot about the process, and how it differed from gold mining. They shared details about how it is mined and how it then goes to the Metallurgical plant for processing. In one of the presentations they had to give to Mine Management, Khathu, even though he was not a Metallurgist himself, but could confidently narrate how the process worked:

"From the mine, the copper ore is then taken to the concentrator, where it is crushed, and after a process of floatation waste is removed and about 46% of it is the precious material. That is then sent, via conveyor belts, to the smelter where the copper mixed with limestone ends up in the furnace. The copper is pressured by air, then oxidised, and poled. The final stage is completed at the refinery where the copper is cast into anodes, through the process of electrolysis."

Motho Fela and Kholofelo's lives had changed dramatically over that period. First it was the *lobolo* negotiations between his delegation and Kholofelo's uncles. Then it was the birth of their baby in September and the weddings that took place over a period spanning six months, from July to December.

The negotiation process brought long lost family members together. On his side he had to track down his uncle Nicholas, whom he wanted to have as his chief negotiator. When he finally found him he was in Bothaville, in the Free State. He requested for them to meet one Sunday afternoon. He was intrigued about what had happened to him, because unlike his father, his face was rough-hewed, and his laid back looks belied his past military career. He showed up in an orange Land Rover, with bumper stickers all over. He knew that that was not going to work on the big day. The flashy land cruiser had to stay behind. He also asked Mnr Koekemoer, who had become a mentor and a coach to him, to be the scribe and assistant to his uncle. For a translator, he asked Kenny who could also be the designated driver, because he knew Kholofelo's village very well. Kenny Phahladire was from the same Mamone Chiefdom. He was familiar with all traditions and customs regarding marriage and the negotiations that came with it.

The event went drama free. It started off very early in the morning, with the *lobolo* negotiations, and then later in the day the traditional wedding. They had arrived in Burgersfort the previous night, so there would be no driving around in the morning. Only key family members and close friends had come with them. There were twelve people in total. His sister could not make it. Travelling from New Zealand would have been expensive - at least that's what she said. Motho Fela wanted it to be a private affair. But that's not how it ended. The second part of it was a big village celebration. There were people from neighbouring villages. They wanted to witness this rare occasion of a local girl being married off into a white family. It had never happened in their region before, and it wasn't about to happen anytime soon. This occasion meant that traditionally Kholofelo was then Motho Fela's wife. But due to the multiplicity of systems that modern Africans live under, the marriage was only going to be official when they registered it at Home Affairs in front of a marriage officer of the court. That would still not be enough. Motho Fela's family wanted them to have a small private wedding at a pristine chapel along the Vaal River in Vanderbijlpark, early December, when the baby was born, where a *predikant* (minister) could bless their union in traditional *Nederduits Gereformeerde Kerk* style.

There was no need for them to go on honeymoon. That's what they had started the year with, in Zanzibar. Kholofelo came back to the mine, after that mid-year break as *mev* (Mrs) Kholofelo du Toit.

A bouncy, baby boy was born in Klerksdorp, at Matlosane Private Hospital. He was given four names, because none of the grandparents wanted to be left out of the joyous moment. His paternal grandfather named him Gerhardus, which in short is Gert. His paternal grandmother named him James, which was her grandfather's name. Then he had two African names from his maternal side – Keorapetse (I prayed for you) and Kegotshofetshe (I am satisfied), which was shortened to *Kego*. They simply called him GJKK, so that no one would feel left out or undermined.

When they finished the programme at GIBS, Motho Fela had had two and half years of communication with Thamaasat University in Bangkok. He had saved up a lot of money over that period, because secretly he had been planning his exit from the mine and from South Africa. He just wanted to finish serving his contractual obligations with the company and leave.

Life was easy and affordable for them. That gave them a chance to build strong cash reserves for themselves. As a married couple they then qualified to stay in a mine-owned, three-bedroom house in Orkney, for free. The house was not far from Kholofelo's old commune at 23 Chesterton Road. They had a full-time, live-in nanny who looked after GJKK. It was an old but well maintained house with a double garage and servant's quarters at the back.

Midnight Express on the Mekong River

The following year, towards the end of January, classes started at GIBS. They went on their first four day stay in Johannesburg. The mine arranged suitable accommodation for them, in such a way that they could bring GJKK and his nanny with them. Classes would start very early in the morning, and they would take only an hour lunch break, and go on again till 19h00, with short tea breaks in between. The programme was an intense process of active learning, which involved rigorous self-evaluation, peer-coaching, and case study work.

After two years of these monthly block release engagements, they emerged with great connections in corporate South Africa; state owned enterprises; business and the NGO sector. Their view of the world was even wider than what they had benefited from working in the continent. One of the biggest benefits for Motho Fela was to form ties with a visiting Professor from the United Nations' owned University for Peace in San Jose, in Costa Rica. She spoke very passionately about the need for human centred design. She impressed upon him the dire need for organisations around the world to find practical and sustainable solutions to complex challenges. Her view was that the best way to deal with complexity, diversity and chaos was for universities to offer more of the design thinking related courses, because those are the tools that will equip leaders with skills to handle abstract concepts.

Motho Fela loved the idea. It tied in well with all his research about Asia, starting with his friend Huang Hu, in Zambia. He felt that it was an act of serendipity. The universe was conspiring in his favour. The stars had aligned perfectly for him. He wasted no time, and applied immediately. Communication with the people at Thammasat University in Thailand was refreshingly easy. There were no language barriers whatsoever.

Motho Fela and Kholofelo resigned exactly a week after they were free of their contractual obligations at the mine. Anushka also resigned and moved overseas. She moved to South India, and stayed with her extended family in Sai Baba Nagar, in Hyderabad.

She was hired by BRICS Bank in Hi-Tech City where she was going to head up a department that was setting up a mining and construction investment unit in Southern Africa. She would be based in India, but would travel to South Africa frequently. Khathu never resigned, but instead was promoted to second in command of East Mine's Planned Engineering Maintenance Division.

The du Toits left South Africa on a work permit that allowed them to work in Thailand for five years, before it could be up for review. They were granted these permits because of their scarce skills. The arrangement was that Motho Fela would study in the afternoons, at Thammasat University, and would teach English at a local high school in Bangkok during the day, for the first two years. Kholofelo found a job at the Siam Council for Geoscience, as a senior researcher investigating the viability of underground water table management systems in South East Asia.

Motho Fela left South Africa one month before his family came over. He flew Kenyan Airways, connecting in Nairobi first to the Middle East in Muscat, and then the following morning to Suvarnabhumi International Airport in Bangkok. This day and half travel experience gave him a glimpse of what being a global player is all about. On the different flights, he met people from all walks of life. He felt a connection with all of them regardless of where they were from, or what they looked like. When he arrived in Bangkok, it was too late for him to take the BTS fast train into the city centre. So he called a cab.

"Sawadi khap" (Hello sir) said the cab driver politely, bowing his head slightly, with his hands together as if he was praying. Motho Fela bowed like the driver, but didn't know what to say in return. He just said "Udee Bangkok Hostel, Phaya Thai". The driver nodded again, and off they went. Hardly an hour and 150TBH later he arrived at his new abode. It was in a quiet part of town, in a residential neighbourhood. The couple who ran the hostel were very helpful. He settled in easily. He loved the fact that the establishment had high speed internet and that they served breakfast in the mornings. Staying there was cheap. The Rand was two and half times stronger than the Thai Baht (TBH). He first paid

for a week's stay - in case he didn't like it. It cost him the equivalent of R700, which was unheard of back home. At the end of the week, he paid for the remaining three weeks before his family would join him.

That first month was for him to take care of the formal accommodation arrangements; sort out all administration issues at work and find a nanny for GJKK. It also gave him time to visit the South African embassy, and introduce himself.

He never cooked throughout the four weeks. Not that he could, anyway. The hostel did not have such facilities for the tenants. He survived on street food. There was plenty of it, almost everywhere. He loved the roast duck, served with sticky rice. When he was tired of it, he would buy chicken wings on skewers. When he really missed a South African taste, he bought roast pork, because it was crispy and salty. Street food was amazingly cheap. A full meal would cost him an average of R25. That included fruits and juice as well.

On his first weekend there, he decided to contact the nearest kayaking club, which he had found through an internet search. He went over, and signed up as a member. This gave him access to the local culture, and gave him an opportunity to make new friends. The club was run by nature conservationists, who had cleaned up a *khlong,* and pumped in fresh water so that they could use it for recreational purposes. They also revived an old waterside hanging market, which supplied fresh produce to the locals. Monthly membership was only the equivalent of R200, and this gave him access to the *khlong* every weekend, plus he qualified for discounts in kayak hire. Ordinary members of the public paid the equivalent of R50 for a two hour hire, but as a member he would get 20% discount. Most of the stalls at the hanging waterside market were social enterprises that were linked to great causes in the community such as taking care of the aged and invalid.

His closest friend, Seramethakun whom he simply called Sera, from the kayaking club organised one day for them to go on a Mekong River overnight boat ride. The Mekong is one of the largest and longest rivers in South East Asia. For this particular boat ride, Sera had invited other expats who were part of his club. He wanted them to meet their new addition to the family. The boat was nothing fancy, but it had all the essentials. There was plenty of food and drinks. There was music, for them to do *karaoke*. There was a sail on top in case it rained. There were toilet facilities downstairs. And the beach seats could roll out and be converted into beds if anyone of them was tired and wanted to sleep.

"Guys we have a new addition to our club. His name is *Motor Fellar*, and he is from Africa. Come on buddy come and introduce yourself." First he explained how his African nickname came about, and corrected the pronunciation. He went on to say, "I am a global citizen. My religion is love. My race is human." As he went back to rejoin the group, he heard one person whispering to another: "…but he is white! How come he is African?"

They had the whole night to themselves. One of the exciting activities they kept themselves entertained with, was to have each one choose a song from the play list which reminded them of home. They would say who they were, and where they came from. Then they would introduce the song, and explain why they had chosen it. When Motho Fela's chance came, he didn't have to introduce himself again, but went straight into his song choice. He selected Johnny Clegg's *Scatterlings of Africa*.

"This song is very close to my heart. It talks about the origins of human kind. To me it says, we all have a common ancestor, who came originally from Africa. It then explains what has happened to us and what we have done with each other, from the time we started getting scattered around the world"

Three weeks into his stay in Bangkok he finally found a two bedroom flat near the BTS Speed Train Service route. It was near the Victory Monument. He loved it because it was not too far from all the city attractions and it was convenient for their daily commute. On the first week of March, his family finally came to BKK and they were reunited. GJKK had grown so much. He went to welcome them from the Suvarnabhumi International Airport.

Lucky enough that afternoon the train was not full. The compartment had enough space for them to sit next to each other comfortably, with their luggage.

Little GJKK was hungry. He could not help it.

To onlookers it was a strange sight – black mother; white father and a mixed race child. It was new to them. Most *farangs* (foreigners) did not look like that.

8. LEADERSHIP DASHBOARD

Shifting From the Balcony Perspective

The real reason for Motho Fela and Kholofelo to leave South Africa, and move to South-East Asia, was to explore what it would be like to escape the tight confines of the skin they were born into. They knew how limiting the South African perspective on identity, race and responsibility was. They wanted something bigger; something more open and liberating. Thailand promised that exposure. It was an awakening that would zip open the trapped souls within their individual skins; to do that they had to jump deep into the rivers of life.

Life at Thammasat's Tha Phra Chan Campus, in Phra Nakhon, was challenging at first for Motho Fela, but as time went on he managed to get into the groove. He attended classes from Monday to Thursday, in the evenings from 18h00 to 21h00, and then again on Saturdays from 08h00 to 16h00. The School of Global Studies, where he had become a student, was a progressive unit of the campus. It had 25 nationalities enrolled in their different programs. Most of them had come in through their work at the United Nations, in different missions around the world. He was the only one who had signed up by himself, from recommendations he got back home. His day job, as a high school English teacher was a walk in the park. He felt he was walking in his mother's shoes. The only difference was that this was high school, and not primary.

Kholofelo on the other hand was having the time of her life. She had made friends in her research unit, and also in the other units at the council. What made it easy for her to be a part of the family, and enjoy the neighbourliness, was the easy-going culture of how people there worked. Similar to her husband's work experience, there were people from many parts of Asia who worked there. She found it easiest to connect with the Indians and Chinese, because they were not completely new for her. South Africa has one of the largest Indian communities in the world. As a student at Wits, she had a lot of contact with the Chinese community of Cyrildene, who ran the Bruma Flea Market and China City in Johannesburg.

Motho Fela's daily routine was such that he would finish teaching at 14h00 and walk home. Then he would catch up with GJKK, while preparing himself for his evening classes. Kholofelo only got home at 16h30, which meant they would only have 30 minutes together, before he hopped on his new motorcycle to head to campus. By the time he got home in the evenings, GJKK would be sleeping. In the mornings, GJKK would be the first one to wake up. They would hear his high pitched voice making sighs and coos, followed by babbles like 'aah-mmm' or 'aaaa –da'. This helped them start their day early, to make time for the commute to work. Then, Kanya, the nanny, would take over from there. Although her name directly translates to *'girl'* in Thai, it is not used in the same South African context where a full grown up woman would be called a *'girl'*, simply because of working as a domestic worker.

Both of them were benefiting from the cross-cultural experiences of their new environment. They spent time listening to stories, and finding out what they could on weekends, so that they would fully be a part of the culture and make friends in the city. Kayaking was something they could only do when it was sunny, and only during the day. They didn't have much to do in the evenings.

Over the three months that they had lived in BKK, their names had morphed to Fela and Felo. They had made a name for themselves as a hip and happening 21st century couple, a living example of what was possible when people crossed the colour barrier. Little did people know the battles they were fighting within themselves.

One Saturday night, they went out to a club called Sing-Sing, to experience the nightlife of the city, with three of their friends – Yunus and his wife Karima who were from India, and Yamamoto from Japan. The club was on the alley of Soi Sukhumvit 45, near the Khlong Tan Nuea in Watthana. It was this big old theatre building that had been converted to an upmarket club mostly frequented by foreign nationals. At the entrance there were scary looking muscular Nigerian bouncers in black uniform, who could dissuade the ne'er do wells just by one word 'stop'. The club had two floors. The ground floor was the main dance area. It was crowded and the air was sweat drenched. So they moved upstairs. The upper level was for the Sing-Sing's VIP patrons. It had a lounge feel to it. There were white sofas, laid out flamboyantly, with fluffy scatter cushions and glass-top coffee tables. There was no dancing going on upstairs. It was mainly classy expats who wanted the relaxed feel, where they could connect with other influential people in BKK, while enjoying the club vibe. As VIPs they loved having their drinks while leaning against the rails, with a clear view of the dance floor below. The owner of the club, former Field Marshall Pridi Setabut, would make time to greet his VIP guests and get to know them a little. That also allowed him to see what was happening on the dance floor, and monitor any behaviour that was unacceptable. There was no way to control the club if he operated from the ground floor. Shifting to the balcony area and VIP section gave him super vision of his entire business.

White Capped Mountain Tops

Felo's work at the Council for Geo-Science exposed her to real issues about the water wars emerging in Asia, and other parts of the world. While people in the west were obsessing about oil, from the Middle East and the West Coast of Africa, many parts of the world were struggling to provide safe drinking tap water. The world was shifting more towards bottled water. This meant there would be pressure on the environment if plastic manufacturing was not complemented by progressive waste management practices.

When Fela was tired of listening to the university's anthem, the *Yung Thong* (Golden Flamboyant), which was played on the speakers in all the campus corridors every Saturday morning before classes began, he would either put on his headphones and listen to South African music or listen to the soothing jazzy tunes of Sadao Watanabe. On Sundays they would go with friends on motorcycles to explore the countryside. They would go through forested farmland, alongside canals and visit ancient Buddhist temples. Beyond the BKK congestion, there was a chance to breathe. The tall buildings would be replaced by small wooden houses. The roads would be narrower. The crowds would be replaced by lush vegetation and trees. They would say hello to the locals on small paddle boats that gave them access to the fruit gardens hanging over the many streams and *khlongs*.

Towards the end of April, there was a public holiday; a very long weekend, starting Wednesday afternoon. They had a full four days to themselves. GJKK was used to life with Kanya. They got along very well together. Felo thought it would be a chance to test what it would be like if she left GJKK with his nanny for a full three days. They organized with friends to travel out of the country to find the source of the Mekong River. The Mekong is a trans-boundary river in Asia that has its basin in Tibet, and then flows for 4 350 km. It runs through China, Myanmar, Laos, Thailand, Cambodia and Vietnam. It is the world's 12th longest river. They had studied the maps. Through her work, Felo had made calls to fellow academics in Tibet to join them on this expedition.

Fela was excited about the trip. The prospect of seeing with his own eyes the point at which science, consciousness and social dynamics meet was a profound experience that he was looking forward to. He wanted to be there and learn about the geo-science and share that learning experience with his geologist wife. He couldn't wait to hear the mythical and historical narratives of how the Mekong had shaped the lives of people at a physical and spiritual level. But even more importantly, in line with his studies on social innovation and leadership, was to learn more about what caused animosity and division amongst the people who lived on either side of the Mekong, from country to country.

The Tibetan researchers had shared notes on the geology of the Mekong, for Felo to go through before coming over, so that she could frame her mind accordingly. She noted three main points that she wanted to learn more about. The first was the fact that unlike her experience with deep level mining issues back at home, the Mekong basin was not a seismically active area. Much of the basin is underlain by the relatively stable continental block. Only the parts that are in Laos and northern Thailand experience frequent earthquakes and tremors that would rarely exceed 6.5 on the Richter magnitude scale. The second point that intrigued her was how the Mekong controlled the course of rivers and the landscapes it carves out. That was because its underlying geological structure is heterogeneous and active. And lastly, unlike large river systems in the world like the Congo, Amazon and Mississippi, the Mekong River does not have dendritic tributary networks that resemble a branching tree.

The flight and all the logistical activities to get them out of Thailand through the Don Mueang Airport to Tibet took half a day. There were two people waiting for them at the airport, and they drove them up the mountainous slopes to the Tibetan Plateau where the air is thinner and the temperature is so cold your nose can drop to the ground from frost bite. Halfway up the mountains, they had to park the Land Rover at one of the researcher's mountain log cabin, and leave all of their luggage there. The only things they were able to take along was camping equipment, water, food supplies, warm clothes and ointment for mosquito bites.

They had to walk up a few kilometres, accompanied by some locals, who served as their mountain guides. They brought six, thick-haired donkeys with to carry the luggage.

As they walked the ravishingly, cold, high grounds of Tibet, where the only sign of human life are the isolated monasteries perched on hanging rock cliffs, Fela and Felo realised that that they had never been so determined or single-minded. They had never followed water the way they did. Even at the mine shaft, following drain water in case you get lost, does not take so much out of you physically and emotionally. They got to the top of one rocky spot, and all of a sudden they could see below them, water cascading down from flat shiny rock beds to the point where the water conglomerated, from which a stream grew. First it was only a trickle. Then it became a narrow stream which bulged into a pond.

Instead of rushing down, to the source of the Mekong River, they decided to stop and soak in all the natural wonder. Each one chose a different spot, where they could sit quietly and write in their journals. Fela's diary entry that afternoon was "....I can safely say, nothing has one single source of origin. The Mekong River basin that I am observing right now, about 300m below where I am sitting, is merely the point at which water flowing from other countless sources come together." They spent an hour there, before they hiked down, leaving their donkeys at the top to graze. As they descended, Felo could see naked rock, layer by layer each telling a story of changing weather patterns over the millions and millions of years of its existence. She could see, touch and feel the geomorphological features normally associated with sediments and alluvial stretches of mature rivers.

This experience had a profound effect on them. It gave them an opportunity to think deeply about the presence of their past, and how everything had unfolded, taking their lives to where they were. They could connect the dots about the present situation they were partaking in, how authentic it was and how much it was drawing out more of who they were in their true natural state. It gave them a glimpse of the presence of the future that was emerging. It reflected the new networks they were part of, the communities they could call theirs and the love they enjoyed with each other and the family they were building together.

On their personal leadership dashboard, they were impressed by all the indicators on display. In terms of how much energy they had available to push forward, taking their careers to the next levels, there were still a lot of possibilities ahead. They were on track as far as their medium-term and long-term goals were concerned. Financially they were in a good space. Life in Thailand was relatively cheap. They only paid 8000TBH in rent, which was just over R3500 a month. Eating out was affordable. A typical meal would cost them just under 900TBH, which was not bad for a family of four. Strategically their careers were leveraged by the relationships they were forming as they went along. In as far as their priorities on spirituality, vitality and cultural exposure they were gaining good momentum. They were evolving into self-actualised individuals, with a heightened sense of self and a broader view of what lay ahead.

The Arrival of Mali

When they climbed back up to their base camp, above the river basin, Fela and Felo decided to sleep in one double layer sleeping bag, under two thick blankets. Body heat is much more effective than any hot water bottle or blanket. Early in the morning they lit a fire so that they could have coffee and rusks for breakfast.

They spent the rest of the morning walking back slowly to the cabin, behind the caravan of donkeys. The walk took up the major part of the morning. Walking down had its own challenges. The gravity pull on the load on their backs, and the cracking of knee joints all added to the physical challenges they faced on their way down. The locals who had accompanied them didn't seem to be having any difficulty at all. They were used to the terrain, and the task of accompanying tourists up the slopes.

When they finally arrived at the cabin, they put together some dry logs and in no time they were wrapped up in blankets, enjoying a warm fire, sipping on steaming hot vegetable soup.

"So how was it guys? What were your main takeaways on this trip?" asked their host. Fela was the first to respond. "I am still pinching myself just to make sure that I am not dreaming. This has been a huge life changing experience for me. I feel like I have now moved to a higher level of being. I have crossed a point of no return. After this I do not see myself being anything close to who I used to be as a man, a father and as an engineer. It has been a great turning point. I am ready to leave behind any limitations that used to hold me back. I want to embrace the future as it is opening up for me one window at a time."

Felo was just as stunned and spoke straight from the heart. "For me this has been a serendipitous rebirth opportunity. My vibrations are up, and I can feel my point of attraction is at its highest. With this level of peace and harmony that I am feeling right now, I am ready and available to take on whatever life throws my way. I can see things clearly now. My geology career is taking on another gear. I am excited about that. I am not even thirty yet but already I can count all these remarkable experiences. I have ticked a lot of items on my bucket list. What more could I ask for? I am surrounded by love. Nothing beats that."

Preparing lunch was an adventure. What do you eat when you are more than 3500m above sea level? Whatever they prepared had to be very high in energy, to keep them warm. The high altitude limited the types of vegetables available for human consumption. Traditional and religious belief also brought another twist to their food choices. In that high altitude another thing that they had to contend with was how long it took to prepare food. Water does not boil fully at such atmospheric pressures. They had to stick to what the locals refer to as 'the four treasures' of their cuisine – *tsampa*, which was roasted barley flour and butter tea, served with high protein meat in egg based noodle soup.

They spent the rest of the afternoon indoors, planning for their early morning trip, which had to go via the Potala Palace and then head back to the airport. There was no way they could go back to BKK and not see the majestic white and red building complex set against grey and green mountains. Spending a few hours at the palace would give them a chance to see Buddha statues, precious sculptures, religious jewellery and all other treasures housed within.

The sheer joy of being on the land where the world's tallest mountain peak is found, was just magical for them. Everywhere they looked they saw groups of pious looking young men clad in flowing garments of many shades of red, with shaved heads. Those were lay Buddhist monks, who dabbled between public and monastic life.

As they reflected on the plane, on their way back to Bangkok, their minds drifted in many directions. It had been such a deeply transformative healing set of experiences. It showed them that they were far removed from where they had started their lives as youngsters growing up in Ga-Mohlala and Fochville. There was nothing like it back home. Home was not even on the same continent, let alone the same country. Their identities had changed. Their names had taken on a new form, a shortened variation that made them a unit, transcending all linguistic and cultural boundaries. Even their son GJKK back in Thailand was opening his young eyes to a new world, where he had a Thai nanny who spoke to him in Thai and English. All of that spoke of how big and how wide their world had expanded.

A month and a half later, on an easy Thursday afternoon, just when Fela was playing with GJKK downstairs on the jungle gym, Felo came home surprisingly early. When they saw her, they both looked up. They saw this very happy woman carrying a bright yellow umbrella. It was blown out, and she held it in such a way that in her tummy area facing them. This made them very curious. When they jumped up to go hug her, a fake scan printout fell out. She closed the umbrella. Fela picked it and asked "What's this?" and Fela playfully said "Hey *wena* (you) Einstein, can't you see it's a 2D picture showing the active morphological formations of the rock features and hydrology in the volcanic mountain of Felo?"

After all the celebrations about the new addition to the family, that night, they agreed that they had to go for a proper scan at a local clinic. The results came, and confirmed that yes they were officially six weeks pregnant. With such information at hand, the main thoughts for Fela were about his additional responsibilities coming up soon. Felo was really a pressure cooker. She had planned all that. She wanted her children to be born close to each other. She didn't like the idea of long gaps in between. Juggling career and family was not going to be easy for both of them, but everything is figure-out-able.

On the 8th of January 2004 a healthy baby girl, weighing in at 3.2kg was born in the first hour after midnight at Bumrungrad International Hospital. They named her Mali. In Thai the name means Jasmine. But when they called back home, to let them know of the good news, and tell them what the baby's name was, they were just as excited. In South Africa, according to many African languages Mali means Money. Family and friends were excited that the little girl was born into money, affluence and a life of abundance on all levels.

Fingers in Many Pies

Raising young children in a foreign country was not a walk in the park. They had to find ways in which their children could learn multiple languages all the same time. Daddy wanted them to be able to speak Afrikaans, while mommy wanted them to speak SePedi and Kanya the nanny spoke to them in Thai. When mommy and daddy played with them together they spoke English. Another twist for the kids was that when mommy and daddy spoke to each other, they spoke in many languages. It was English, Afrikaans and when they were really excited and felt like they were really missing home, they would speak to each other in Fanagalo. All of that was funny galore as a drama playing out. The kids at their age knew the difference between the various sounds and clicks. But later when they had grown up a little, and started interacting with other children in the kindergarten, they started speaking clearly in two languages – English and Thai.

It was a marvel for Fela and Felo to observe their children integrating fully into Thai society. They cushioned the bumpy bits of the social experiences by making sure that in their circle of friends they had both Thai and other foreign nationals. Their children played together, and even went to the same schools. The children developed amazing language abilities. The ability to switch between different sounds, words, concepts, grammatical structures and social norms accelerated their brain development. It enhanced their working memory, problem solving, and planning abilities. Growing up multilingual gave them unfair advantages, like being aware of other people's cultures and being tolerant to their points of view. Those were traits that Fela and Felo wanted their children to learn very early in life.

By the time GJKK was five years old, they had made big plans about what their next chapter in life looked like. Fela was finished with his studies at Thammasat's Centre for Global Studies. He was then working with the university, driving an international project that explored ways in to reduce the environmental effects of plastic waste in dams, rivers and oceans. They had formed a social enterprise that was incubated within the university, for access to research facilities while it sustained itself financially. He worked with academics in East Africa, Canada, the US, South America and Southern Africa.

His new role involved a lot of travelling, and spending time away from his wife and kids. It was always tricky sometimes when he was working in Southern Africa, in countries such as Mozambique, to decide who he would visit if he took a quick flight into Johannesburg. Driving to Burgersfort to say hello to Felo's parents or to drive to Fochville. So what he would do most of the time would be to call his brother-in-law Thabang, who was then working in Pretoria as a government official, to come and fetch him from the airport. Their first stop would be Fochville, to see how his parents were doing and to show them pictures of the children. Then they would take the long drive to Burgersfort for a sleepover at Ga-Mohlala. Thabang didn't have a problem taking time off from work at short notice, because the culture in government was laid back, no one really checked on him.

The area that Fela loved travelling to the most was Costa Rica. That was where the UN's University for Peace Executive Education Campus was located, in San Jose. They did a lot of collaborative work with UPEACE. A lot of research output, in the field of sustainability and environmental change, was found there and shared with the rest of the world. They were a home away from home for him. At UPEACE he was a part of a community of progressive thinkers and change makers who were shaping the world in ways unseen and unheard of.

Felo never made any changes to her job. She was very happy at the Council for Geo-Science. The only thing that had changed was her focus areas. Her studies were more on water pollution and climate change. Her research outputs were used throughout Asia to advise governments on sustainable ways in which they could deal effectively with intense, frequent and prolonged droughts and floods. There were serious environmental issues they were tackling. The air quality indices in most parts of Asia were dismal and getting worse in most parts. South East Asia was facing an acute public health emergency due to water and air quality. Their challenge was not just to come with solutions on how to curb these problems, but also to make sure their view was not obscured by the main incipient environmental catastrophe – lack of access to clean water. It was a potential source of future conflicts within the region, and other parts of the world. In their work they had found that there was only 3% fresh water available for human consumption and most of it was not accessible because it was locked up in glaciers. From 1960, the amount of available fresh water per capita had declined by more than half, leaving well over 40% of the world's population facing massive water stress.

9. FACE IT TILL YOU MAKE IT

The Calabash

The ear penetrating sound of the *vuvuzelas*, during the 2010 FIFA World Cup, echoed strongly across the globe. It was a clarion call for unity, for love and for redefining the essence of being human. That call was heard loud and clear in Sadiola's street food markets, in Mali. It was felt passionately by dhow paddlers in Dar es Salaam, in Tanzania. It spoke to the hearts and minds of the mine workers in Orkney, here in South Africa. It awakened the imagination of Kayak Club members in *khlongs* throughout Thailand. But most certainly, it evoked deep emotions in the du Toit household near Victory Monument in Bangkok, especially that unforgettable moment when Simphiwe Tshabalala made magic with his searing left foot goal strike in the opening match against Mexico in the calabash shaped Soccer City stadium.

Fela was glued to the screen, when that magical moment happened. He had GJKK next to him, while Mali was on his lap. Felo had done a great job creating an atmosphere that would resemble a typical soccer match day back home in South Africa. They invited a few friends over. The flat was draped with big South African flags, and other memorabilia could be seen all over the place. They had bought twelve matching straw hats at the Chatuchak market, the previous weekend, to give to everyone as a welcome gift when they came to share the moment with them. The tiny flat was packed to capacity. There was hardly space to move around. Felo and Fela wore matching bright gold and green t-shirts, with the words "Feel it, it's here" in front. The mood was high-spirited. They didn't have to worry about their neighbours complaining about the noise, because they had written letters to all of them more than a month before South Africa's first global soccer extravaganza.

If you were a fly on the wall, you would be impressed to see the United Nations represented, in all its glory and warmth. Their

Chinese and Indian friends, Hu, Yunus and Karima, were there. So was Fela's kayaking friend, Sera, who came with his wife and their two young daughters. They also had two of Fela's colleagues from the Centre for Global Studies - Juan from Mexico and Antonio from Spain, who both came with their local girlfriends.

"What do you guys like more, watching the game on TV or at the stadium?" asked Felo, trying to make small talk. Antonio responded, without looking at Felo, because every second of the game was electrifying: "Nothing beats the communal atmosphere in the stadium. The buzz all around you. The air. The ticket stub you can stick in your scrap book to prove that you were there. If I had things my way, I would be in Johannesburg right now. Forget about water and plastic wars for a while".

His girlfriend didn't agree, "....How can the comfort of home be less enjoyable than hard plastic chairs? The drunk guys behind you, shouting all sorts of racial slurs. The long lines in the toilets. Lost cell phone signal. *Naaah* not for me, sorry"

Such was the connectedness they felt with each other, as they watched that match and the other important matches together in the du Toit household and in other public places around the city of smiles, Bangkok. The most memorable one was the final, which was played exactly a month later on the 11th of July 2010, between Spain and Netherlands. It was an enthralling and pulsating match to watch. A lot had happened over that period leading up to that day. It was the 31st day of back to back soccer magic, happening from city to city, throughout South Africa. That was the 64th match to be played, in the nine venues that had hosted the beautiful game. A total of 599 players from 32 teams had partaken in the making of history, scoring a total of 144 goals. That one goal scored on that day by Vicente del Bosque's men became the 145th one for the 2010 FIFA World Cup.

The moment when Mandela appeared, in the calabash, before the final, delighted the crowds all over the world. At the end, when Spain won, their victory was not just a victory for Europe but for Africa as well. South Africa had hosted one of the most memorable soccer tournaments ever. The event had given Africa a chance to shine. It helped the world see that Africa is not a dark continent, it never was, and it will never be. There is only 14.3 km separating Africa and Europe, at their closest points. It is at the Strait of Gibraltar, which separates Spain and Morocco. When Andres Ineasta secured Spain's spot in the world soccer record books, by scoring that goal in the 116th minute against Netherlands, Fela stood up, with his heart pounding heavily in his chest *'dum dum dummm dummmm'* and said, "That's it guys! We're moving back home"

It would be another five months before the du Toit's finally left South East Asia for good, and headed back home to South Africa. Fela's announcement, surprising as it was, delighted Felo. It was a sad moment for Kanya, because it meant she would have to look for a new job. She had grown very close to the kids. Her boss, Felo, was like a sister to her. It broke her heart that they were emigrating. It was also a big decision for Felo, because over the last eight years, her work at the South East Council for Geo-Science had brought a great deal of stability to her life and had exposed her to great minds from around Asia, and the world at large. For the kids, it was a big scary idea. They had never been to Africa. They had seen pictures, and had talked to their grand-parents, and cousins over the phone and video calls on Skype. Bangkok was all they knew. They would miss *khao neaow mamuang,* their mango and sticky rice favourite, and the sweet and tangy noodle dish of *pad thai,* which they loved because of the crunchy peanuts, sugar and prawns. Fela could not wait to be home, to host *braais* every weekend, and tell old friends stories about his travels, while catching up on current affairs.

Mr Angazi

The country they left in 2002 was totally different when they came back in 2010. With the world cup over, and the honeymoon air gone, it was back to reality for South Africa. The country was under the third democratic administration. Mandela had long retired. The African philosopher king president, Thabo Mbeki, had also relinquished power. South Africa was now two years into an era where the lines between state and party were slowly but surely being blurred. This produced all sorts of new breed denialists; chancers; opportunists and a growing class of elitist pseudo-politicians, whose idea of money and power was to flaunt their ill-gotten wealth and flashy German cars.

The du Toits had acquired many possessions in Thailand, and from their global experiences. It was all shipped home, to be collected six weeks later at City Deep, Johannesburg's logistics hub. On the flight, they carried the valuables they could not be separated from. One such item was the gold plated statue of the Buddha, which they wanted to find a spot for in the Zen garden they hoped to make. Fela kept it in his hand luggage. They wondered about the condition of their old stuff, which had been locked away all these years in Fela's parents' garage in Fochville.

When they finally arrived at what was now called OR Tambo International airport, they were most anxious about their luggage. They knew anything could have happened during the two connecting flights they had been on, over the 32 hours. So they rushed to the carousel, to collect their bags. Out of the six bags they had checked in at Suvarnabhumi International, only four showed up. Fortunately, Felo had tagged all their bags before they left, and had taken photos showing what they looked like inside. She even had details about which items were brand new and what their value was. She handled everything with fastidious care. So she was calm. They went to the baggage claim office upstairs.

"*Sawubona baba* (Hello sir), we would like to report missing luggage. We have all the details with us here. Will you be able to locate them?"

The claim handler responded with an unapologetically dull "*angazi*", meaning "*I do not know*" in Zulu. Felo took one breath in, one breath out. "What do you mean you don't know? Are you suggesting that it is not possible for you to know how to locate our bags?" Unperturbed, mr Angazi just said, "it depends on what really happened to your bags. It's possible that they are missing, or got mixed up with the luggage of the next flight coming in or they were lost in a connecting flight somewhere else. So, *angazi*".

It was a rude welcome for the du Toits. Felo then asked "who should we talk to then, because clearly you do not seem to have much useful information?" The gentleman just laughed in a ridiculing way, as if what he really wanted to say was "you need to adjust, this is South Africa, not Europe or wherever it is you have been". He told them, he was the person they had to talk to, and there was no one else on that shift more senior than him.

They filled in a claim report, and took all the details for follow-up. For the address, they gave details of Fela's family home in Fochville, which was where they were going to stay for the first three months in South Africa, while settling in. It was disappointing to have to deal with an airline that failed to hold up their end of the bargain. Nothing much had changed since their first experience close to a decade prior to that. In fact things were worse. Ironically, the airport complex had gone through a beautiful face lift. There were a lot of new facilities. It had a first world feel to it. The legacy of the world cup was such that there were a lot of top class facilities, not just in Johannesburg, but all over the country. The thing that had regressed was the service and the attitude of the people working in those establishments.

Eventually, they came out of the international arrivals section into a vast public lounge. They were overwhelmed by all the family members who came to welcome them. From Fela's side, it was the usual three – his parents, and their driver. But, from Felo's side it felt like the whole Ga-Mohlala village had come through. They were so happy to see them. As they walked through, with their trolleys, they found themselves being grabbed and hugged by family from all angles. There was loud singing of church songs, led by Aunty Betty, who brought her *stokvel ladies* all the way from Mamelodi. Thabang arrived with friends from work, and an unusually friendly hugger, who was never introduced to them, but who had a guilty look on her chubby face. Felo's parents were arguing about who was going to hold Mali first. She had grown into a loveable little lady, with brightly coloured twists in her hair.

The happy crowd then moved upstairs to the food court, where they took over like a swarm of bees. It was late summer after all. That kind of social propagation was temporary, and could therefore be excused.

Front Stabbing

They spent the whole afternoon at the airport, breaking bread with family, and rekindling old love ties the best way they knew how. They agreed that over the weekend they would visit Ga-Mohlala, where a huge welcome back feast was prepared for them, but in the meantime they could spend their first few days in Fochville. Surprisingly enough the old VW Microbus, vintage as it had become, was still holding up. They drove in it, and were happy to share stories with the kids about their memories. They meandered through the R24, then the N3, and slipped away onto the N12 west towards Soweto. They did not mind how long the trip took. Stopping twice along the highway to fill up with water, to cool the radiator was not an issue for them at all. All they cared about was just being back home, sharing the joy of being united as a family and smelling the fresh summer air of the Highveld.

Along the highway, they were shocked to see so many informal settlements that had mushroomed almost everywhere they looked. There were tiny brick houses, with large solar panels on top, that looked like their roofs could cave in at any time because of how heavy the panels were. The off-ramps were announced by names of dead, anti-apartheid struggle stalwarts whose legacy was preserved by naming squatter camps after them. Those were not the only contradictions and ironies they noticed. Time and again, they had to change lanes or drive more towards the curb, because they had to make way for convoys of black SUVs, that would whizz through, breaking all the traffic rules. Fela's parents told them it was the notorious *blue light brigade* which had become a common sight on the highways. Apparently politicians' busyness was more important than the safety of other road users. Presumably their meetings either finished late or started early;

what else could justify their fast and furious driving? Being in a rush was a new symbol of power and influence.

The culture of South Africa had changed since they had left, as had the language. There was strange new terminology everywhere they went. Prisons were no longer jails, they were correctional services centres. School children were no longer called students, but learners. If you witnessed a fisticuff at a club, which ended with the two guys stabbing each other, you could no longer just say they stabbed each other. You would say, "they allegedly stabbed each other". The president was referred to as u*baba*, not a head of state, but more like a father; a patriarch everybody could relate to, or the uncle they never had.

Fela noticed this even more when he attended business meetings, with people in state owned enterprises or municipalities. They spoke with caution. Their words were brief, and reserved. The holding back, felt like there was a heavy cloud of fear and suspicion hanging over every meeting. It made him uneasy, unable to connect freely with people. Decisions were hard to reach. The impression he got was that even simple matters were decided by some secret body somewhere else, away from the meeting rooms. There was much secrecy, even hostility. Red tape was the order of the day. In Asia he had been used to swift and decisive action, where leaders took responsibility for what they did and had full power to do so without fear of reversal or reprieve.

"Your verbal diarrhoea is not going to get you anywhere in this country" said one municipal manager in the Vaal, at a meeting where he was presenting an idea that would see dams being created along the Vaal river, to preserve rain water and prevent flooding during the rainy season. What he thought was a harmless remark about how officials didn't seem concerned that when the river burst its banks during heavy rains, shack dwellers lost their homes, landed him in serious trouble.

All he had said was "I now understand fully why De Nial is the longest river in Africa, and the Con Go is the widest and deepest". When the municipal boss took a swipe at him, it cut right through, to the core of his being. To Fela, it didn't make sense why a public servant, who had sworn an oath to "...serve ,promote and maintain the highest standards of professionalism and ethics in all we do, with *Ubuntu* and *Batho Pele* as our ever-present watchwords." could react like that. Those words were unfortunately only in the Official Pledge by the Members of the Public Administration of South Africa, in paper form, practiced rarely in real life.

Talking to Bricks

Fela's biggest concern at that stage of his life was sustainable provision of water and dignified sanitation for all. He was a product of the mines, and had grown up in the agricultural town of Fochville that was surrounded by deep level mines. He knew how much water was guzzled by mines and agricultural cultivation systems. His work abroad gave him first-hand experience of what happens when water sources start dwindling.

In Asia he had seen how the cultivation of rice was at the center of academic debates, and how it even led to conflict in some nations. Evidence showed that in order to produce a kilogram of beef, five times more water was needed than a kilogram of rice, and 130 times more than a kilogram of potatoes. In rural India, he had seen girls walking long distances daily to collect drinking water. In Maharashtra, in particular, there were villages where the local wells had run dry; households had to designate a child to be on full-time water collection duty. Water stress in those areas had caused major disruption of livelihoods and undermined human dignity. He didn't want the same for South Africa. He knew the country and the region had similar challenges, and it was time to craft lasting solutions.

The depletion of ground water and the subsequent environmental degradation contributed directly to climate change. In South Africa what made the situation worse was the fact that there were lifestyle and industrial excesses that put pressure on water sources. The Vaal river was a prime example. The land along both its banks, across the provinces of Mpumalanga, Gauteng, the Free State and

North West, had long been long been targeted for acquisition. Foreign investors, who go around the world buying up fertile ground on the wetlands, had not left the Vaal alone for its economically viable provision of high agricultural yield, biogenetic value and industrial water supply. It made sense for Fela to join those who wanted to avert the coming water wars.

The main challenge he faced, more often than not, was that those who had been entrusted with developing policy and championing the agenda on what had to be done regarding water and sanitation, were more interested in their own internal party political squabbles than the real assignment they had in their hands. It really frustrated Fela, and he often discussed this with his wife at home. Felo had been lucky in that her research career had not been disrupted. She had secured a similar job at the Pretoria-based South African Council for Geo-Science, where she was tasked with setting up a new research unit that would look into bigger environmental issues around water, the environment and weather patterns not just in South Africa, but the Southern and East African corridor all the way up to Kenya. She was a great pillar of strength in Fela's life. She provided him with wise counsel because their work had finally been aligned.

Towards the end of 2011, on GJKK's 11th birthday, they both received invitations to be a part of a panel discussion that was going to be hosted by GIBS Alumni Association, which would be broadcast live on national television. The topic for the day was "There are major threats to our water systems: But, are they overstated?" They loved it, and signed up right away. They would each be representing their different organisations, and speak independently of each other. It augured well for their individual local career development. They loved the fact that their work was being noticed out there. Their intention was also to see if they could use footage from the media coverage to then leverage on it for further participation in similar discussions abroad. Participating in an evening event was not much of an issue for them, because they had set up a strong support system, in their new home in Midrand. So on that night, Thabang and his significant other were babysitting. Thabang loved his uncle duties, and spending time with his nephew and niece gave him and Dimples a chance to practice the parenthood games.

When they arrived at the auditorium at GIBS they were surprised to see such a strong contingent of the blue light brigade, accompanied by massive media presence. It was only then that it dawned on them they were going to be on the same panel as the Minister of Water Affairs and Sanitation, the Honourable Princess and Heir Apparent of the BaPedi Kingdom and Sekhukhuneland in particular, the former commissar of the underground armed struggle, *Isithwalandwe* Doctor Reverend Mamone Mamone the 8th. Men and women clad in crocodile skins and fox hides were gathered around her, but Fela could still see her because of her distinctive peacock feathered hat. She seemed to be in high spirits. The mood around her was jovial yet dignified. While the rest of the people were filing in, the event coordinator and her assistants were outside briefing the panellists on protocol matters and how they were going to be ushered in.

Pomp and ceremony was not something that Fela and Felo were used to. For them the most important thing was the topic at hand, and the potential solutions they could bring to the table. But then they had to obey local ways of doing things. When the ceremonial theatrics had been taken care of, and it was time to start the process, they were delighted to find that the adjudicator for the discussion was former CNN weather reporter, Kinky Jacobs. Besides the minister, there were two other panellists. On the extreme right was the president of the Jukskei River Shack Dwellers Association, Mr Perseverance Mugabe. Sitting between Fela and Felo, was an analyst from the Johannesburg Media Research Foundation, Felicia Gaylord.

In her opening remarks, Felicia focused on the need for responsible reporting by the media. Her views, coming from a media person, were refreshing and educational at the same time. She spoke about how reports were often exaggerated or out of touch with reality on the ground. She cited a claim about how media had reported irresponsibly about the garbage patch in the oceans. Journalists reported that there was six times more plastic than zooplankton in the North Pacific Ocean. Those journalists, in compiling that report, had used second hand data that had been used for other purposes and therefore misquoted it. was Zooplankton was five times more abundant than plastic, but plastic weighed six times more, suggesting that plastic posed a bigger threat in ocean water.

That really got the minister excited. She was not friends with the media, but she knew how important they were for her public relations machine. The only thing for her was to find a balance about when to criticise the media and when to bring them with when she wanted to spin something important.

As the discussions heated up, Felo weighed in with a less sensational but fact based perspective, which really impressed Fela.

"I've devoted a fair amount of my life to studying marine ecosystems. In my research work, I ended up being diverted to the effects of plastics in the sea and rivers. One of the critical questions that I have been asking over the years has been, 'why is plastic perceived to be such a significant threat?' That is but one out of so many critical questions we need to ask ourselves regarding our lifestyle choices, industrial work and public water usage. Recently it is quite common to find newspaper headlines saying 'An Average Person could be Ingesting 5g of Microplastics per Week'. As the honourable minister has highlighted the need for staying away from alarmist reporting, I also agree with my fellow panellist Felicia here that we need to be sober minded when reading such articles. We have to approach them with a clear filter in our minds in order to discern between what is factual and what is sensationalist commercially driven behaviour on the part of media. I find it highly irresponsible to suggest that human ingestion of water borne plastics is in the region of 2000 micro-plastic particles per week. The value of 5g per week was actually based on a WWF estimate of the size of micro-plastics in aquatic environments, which is 2.8g. That makes it about the size of a sesame seed. That doesn't seem plausible. We'd notice if we consumed 250 sesame seeds in our drinking water every day"

There was a big applause when Felo finished talking. The audience was impressed by her ability to translate what would otherwise have been heavy abstract concepts for the uninitiated listener to comprehend. The points she had made gave comfort to a lot of people.

When they drove back home, they spoke about how much public discussions were a platform for public officials to present a face that made people believe they really cared about the issues on the ground, and they had no problem being challenged directly by those who did not agree with them. But being in the same panel, and enjoying the privilege of what was whispered up on stage, far from the audience's range, were scary comments contrary to what they said when they looked up and smiled in front of the cameras.

Fela was particularly impressed with Perseverence, because he spoke about issues that affected him and his family directly. He lived on the banks of the Jukskei River on the outskirts of the Alexandra Township in Johannesburg. His plea was more around the need for media, academics and politicians to handle these matters with heightened sensitivity to the dignity of the people directly affected by these issues. That is what impressed Fela about him. The question of respect takes away the fictitious handling of the discussions, because it brings in the human and life aspect to it. The ever present sway towards showing off on how abstract these discussions could be handled was his main concern, because he knew how that did not help anyone, but was more about the ego of those engaged in the discussions not the people on the ground who desperately needed the practical solutions. The evening had been well spent, and they had made great contacts with other activists and change makers from across different fields and persuasions. Their position on the national water dialogue was secured. Finally their work was being recognized by the right people.

Third Moment to Pause

1. What are your anxieties and motivating factors for training and development?
2. What is your level of adaptability, especially in foreign social spaces?
3. What keeps you grounded, and deeply connected to your true self?
4. How are you freeing yourself from narrow and shallow vision, to big picture thinking?
5. In your thirst and hunger for new knowledge and skills, what extremes will you go to?
6. How are you making a contribution towards something bigger than yourself?
7. What is your appetite for adventure, high activity and living in the now?
8. When dealing with people who are not logical, what energy do you switch to?
9. What's your tolerance for frank and direct immediate feedback?
10. When you can't get your point across, what do you do? Do you detach and be aloof?

SECTION 4: MIRROR (CONTEXT)

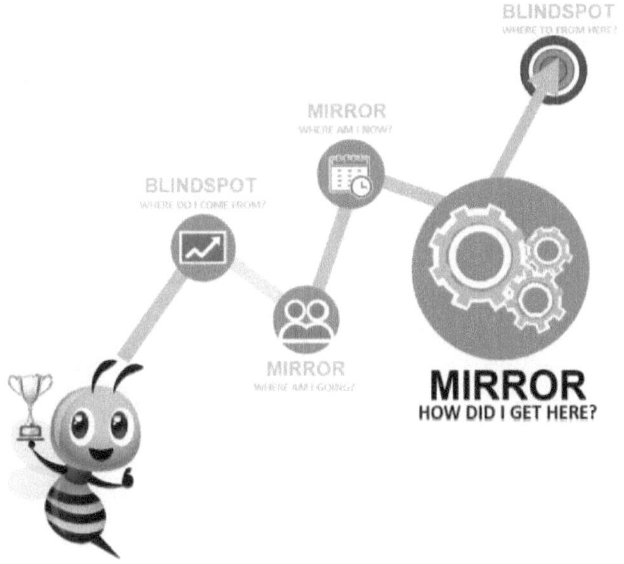

"If you don't understand, ask questions. If you're uncomfortable about asking questions, say you are uncomfortable about asking questions and then ask anyway. It's easy to tell when a question is coming from a good place. Then listen some more. Sometimes people just want to feel heard" **Chimamanda Ngozie Adiche**

10. CHAOTIC ITERATIONS

A Letter from the Big Powers That Be

Scarcely a month after the much publicized event at GIBS, Fela received a rather unexpected email from the office of the Minister of Water and Sanitation. When he opened the attachment, he found that it was a signed official letter. On top, it had his full name, written in fine calligraphy, which was so impressive that it looked like it had been written by a master craftsman, by hand. He felt so special. He had never received a special letter like that before. The letters 'G' and 'T' of his name and surname were accentuated with long feather-like tails. He hastened to read it right away.

It said:

"Dear Mr Gerhardus du Toit,

The Hon. Minister of Water and Sanitation would like to invite you to her official residence in Pretoria. The details are as follows:

Address: 79 Steve Biko Road

WATERKLOOF

0010

Gauteng Province, South Africa

Date: 16 November 2011

Time: 18h00

RSVP, Ms Shamilla Gupta, Chief of Staff in the Office of the Honourable Minister"

He was excited, and anxious at the same time. He just didn't know how to feel. He quickly searched his pockets for his phone. When he got it, he couldn't decide who to call first. His father? His wife? His mother? Or perhaps Thabang, his brother-in-law, because he was more familiar with how government worked? His personal assistant, Patience, who was sitting across the room at another desk, realized that something big had just happened. When she asked him what was going on, he simply asked her to come and have a look for herself. She was so happy about the news. It was comforting for her to see that their work was gaining momentum. To her it meant that her job was secure. It had been a struggle for her to convince her elder sister that she was taking an administrative job with a man who was working from home, running an international organization. It just didn't make sense to her and their family back in Zululand. The letter changed those insecurities.

They still didn't know what the minister was inviting him for. There were no details about what exactly she wanted to discuss. Judging by how the letter was designed, it looked like an event invitation. But when he read it, it sounded more like the minister had some serious water related matters she wanted to discuss with him. It scared him that the meeting was going to be at her official residence. He just didn't know what to make of it. Her office would have been better. After all he had to RSVP to the chief of staff in the office of the minister. He called his wife, and told her the great news. She was so delighted to hear what had just happened. She couldn't wait until she was home that evening to hear all the details. His mother was just as delighted. He left a message for his father, because he was told that he was outside tending to the bees, in one of the big hives in the orchard. Thabang was not very helpful. All he said was, "….don't worry about it. Just go. Probably you guys will have dinner together and a bit of wine, so that she gets to know you. She loves her wine." He didn't say anything about the formal etiquette or any of the protocol stuff. And also, he never guided him on how to respond to the email.

Fela took almost an hour to come up with the right words to put in his RSVP email. His palms were sweating, and the pores on his skin opened up. He could see his arm hair, near his wrist standing on end. Time and again, he would wipe his brow. When that didn't seem to work, he would stand up and pace the room for a minute or two. And then finally, he pulled himself together, and sat down.

Patience was having a lot of fun watching her boss being so uncertain. She loved it. It showed a side of him that confirmed he was human after all. Not this highly acclaimed international water activist and academic.

"Dear Ms Shamilla Gupta,

This letter serves to confirm that yes, indeed, I would love to meet with the Honourable Minister as per the details contained in the official communication received from your office.

Yours sincerely,

Mr Gerhardus du Toit"

Patience was looking over his shoulder as he was writing that letter. She was so close, he could even hear her breathe.

"Fela, why don't you also conclude the letter by saying it is from the Chief of Staff of the Office of the CEO of Waterwise Futurwise (Pty) Ltd?"

But Fela just laughed, and she went back to her desk. For the rest of the afternoon, the mood was great in the office. As a pleasant surprise, Felo came back home earlier than usual that afternoon. She had been doing field work, and didn't have to drive to the office when she finished. She found Fela in a celebratory mood. The kids were already back from school. Uncle Linda, their local school transport guy, had taken care of that. As it was their daily ritual, they made green tea, and went to sit outside in the garden. In that way they could catch up on how their day was, while enjoying the calm sounds of the water cascading down their miniature version of what they had seen at the Mekong River basin in Tibet. The koi fish in the pond would pop their mouths out near the broad water-lily leaves. He narrated the whole story to her, and didn't leave any details out. She was really excited about what that meeting could do for his career, and offered to come along with him.

Creating International Loops and Nodes

They had exactly four weeks to wait before the big day with the minister. There was not much to prepare on their side. Patience sent emails to their contacts overseas, at the United Nations in Switzerland; at Thammasat University's Centre for Global Studies; at the University for Peace in Costa Rica and the Makerere University in East Africa. They hoped to prime their contacts on the latest developments since their return to South Africa, to position themselves for possible collaboration opportunities. They were deliberately solidifying links in order to be proactive and on top of things.

In the four weeks they managed to get official letters of intent, from all the institutions, stating that they were ready and available to work with them on practical solutions for development, management and preservation of water sources. They were all on official letterheads, signed by key people from each organization.

The letters of intent were accompanied by non-disclosure agreements to protect the confidential information contained in the concept documents that Fela's company had presented to them.

Eventually the much anticipated November 16th came. Fela put on his best suit and tie that day, and made sure he shaved properly. He even clipped his nose hair. He drove up the N1 from Midrand to Pretoria. His first stop was the University of South Africa, at the South African Council for Geo-Science, to pick up mev. Kholofelo du Toit.

She had been waiting for him all afternoon. After lunch, the ladies at her office had taken her out to buy a formal ladies suit and formal shoes. The last thing she wanted was to show up at the minister's official residence looking like she had been working with rats in the lab. She had to look authoritative. She had arranged with security to leave her car in the basement, and come back to pick it up later that evening.

They had no problems with traffic, they drove along the back roads of suburban Pretoria. They arrived twenty minutes early. They did not want to keep the minister waiting; provision had to be made for protocol or security issues at the gate. Felo quipped that, "...who knows, we might be subjected to all sorts of security screening. Just be prepared. They might even check us for foot and mouth disease, hahaahaha". And Fela said, "I am ready for anything. Hahahahaaa. I wouldn't mind. Even if they check us for swine flu."

At the gate, there was none of that. They filled in the register, while a thorough check of the car for weapons and so on, was conducted. Then there was a call to the main house, which was answered by an official sounding voice, that said "Let them in". When they drove up towards the huge Tuscany villa they could already feel the dignified aura of the residence. The palm trees lining the single lane driveway made them feel like they were on Hollywood's Sunset Boulevard. They parked the car in the visitor's parking area, and walked up to the already open main door.

The chief of staff, stood there with a broad smile on her face, and said "Welcome. Come on in," signalling them inside with her hand. They followed her slowly. There was so much to feast their eyes on. The entrance hall had animal trophies on one wall, and a huge mirror on the other. One trophy was that of an *Inyala* antelope, with long sharp twisted horns almost a metre long. Felo thought to herself, "What sort of animal lover keeps so many trophies? What does she do with the horns? Does she pull them out in case of an intruder, and say to security 'Don't worry I have this covered" like a martial arts ninja in an old karate movie? What if all those eyes were really cameras for big brother to watch everything going on in the minister's house?" Before she could share her paranoia with Fela, they found themselves in a grand dining room, with a twenty two seat table. They wondered if there would be others joining them. The setting made Fela think of Da Vinci's painting of the last supper between Jesus and his disciples.

As they were about to sit down, the chief of staff introduced herself informally as Shamilla. She said nothing about her surname. The minister then walked in, accompanied by her husband, and two bodyguards. They all stood up, and greeted her. They did what they had learned in Thailand. They put their hands together as if they are about to pray, bowed slightly down, and moved their foreheads towards the tips of their thumbs. This fascinated the minister. As they exchanged pleasantries, she asked them about it. They explained it to her that they had learned to do this in the east where it was a way to show respect to high ranking leaders, priests and royalty. This led to them introducing who they were; how they had met at Wits; their work on the mines; their international study programme and life overseas; their recent return home and their shared passion for community water and sanitation.

The minister liked the sound of all of it, because it supported the vision she had presented to the president and cabinet in Cape Town, after taking up her ministerial position in June that year, following the cabinet reshuffle.

She wanted to establish a water and sanitation advisory board. It would allow her to identify community based organizations with concrete programs to address the nation's water needs. She told Fela how impressed she was, at the event they had participated in together, by his grasp of the issues, especially his concerns about threats of future water wars,. She asked Fela what appealed to him most, being a member of the board or creating content to support the work of her department.

As the welcome drinks were served, Felo remembered the wine bottle they had brought for the minister, which she had forgotten in the car. She decided to leave it there, not sure whether it might be seen as a bribe rather than an honest courtesy.

"Ma'am I am honoured by your kind words. I admire the vision you have for the department. It brings a great deal of hope and confidence to hear what you have in mind. I am happy to support that vision. But first, I would need to learn more about it. I would need to study the details. But, right away, I can safely say I see myself and my team contributing more meaningfully on the part of creating content to enhance the delivery processes at community level. I value my independence, and believe I would be most useful to the department if my company had a role as an independent services provider"

The minister listened carefully. She could tell that Fela was no pushover. On one hand, she liked his principled stance; on the other, she was concerned that his choice of words suggested she might try to 'capture' him.

Working with Perseverance

At the end of January in 2012, government advertised a tender in the Sunday Times.

It read:

INVITATION TO TENDER:

REQUEST FOR PROPOSALS FROM ACCREDITED SERVICE PROVIDERS TO DELIVER A CUSTOMISED INTERNATIONAL EXECUTIVE DEVELOPMENT PROGRAMME (SOUTH AFRICAN QUALIFICATIONS AUTHORITY NQF LEVEL 9) FOR EXECUTIVES AND SENIOR MANAGERS AT THE DEPARTMENT OF WATER AND SANITATION AND ITS AGENCIES.

Fela cut it out, and gave it to Patience on Monday morning. When they read the details, they found it involved a lot of work. Section 6, of the terms and conditions was particularly challenging. It stipulated that:

"The IEDP has six overarching components:

6. 1.   A group of high-impact, cross-industry high potential leaders working together;

6. 2.   Foundation competencies and team competencies such as critical thinking, personal mastery, effective communications, group dynamics and team effectiveness as well as industry and business knowledge such as supply chain management and innovation;

6. 3.   A complex and urgent business or industry challenge which participants research and investigate throughout the process in syndicate teams. This hones their critical thinking and team effectiveness skills as well as cultivating an external perspective. Findings and recommendations of this action learning project are

presented to a senior industry panel at the programme conclusion;

6. 4.	In-market learning meetings with external stakeholders/industry practitioners to promote outside-in thinking and progress business challenge recommendations in both South Africa and abroad;

6. 5.	Structured reflection and knowledge capture embedded in the programme are regular reflection sessions as a cohort and in smaller groups as well as well as structured effort to capture the collective knowledge gained from the programme;

6. 6.	Personal assessments and action coaching. The IEDP uses assessments tools and action learning coaching to ensure participants are optimizing their personal insights and development.

When they were clear about what it entailed, they called Perseverance Mugabe for a meeting at their Midrand office. Because Alexandra Township was only 15 minutes' drive from them, he agreed to come over. While they were waiting for him to join them later that afternoon, Fela drove over to Pretoria to collect the tender document and the forms from the Department's national office. They met with Perseverance, and discussed the requirements of the tender. Perseverance said he was in, and would help them put together their bid for the tender.

"You see Fela, when these people say this has to be an international program, they mean it cannot have anything African. By *abroad*, they exclude all countries in the continent. I know them. We will win this tender if we present a solid bid with verifiable international connections"

In that way Perseverance proved that he was going to be a valuable contributor to the process of putting together their bid. Fela wanted to assemble a team that was going to help his company before the tender bid, and then later when they had won the tender. It wasn't a question of 'if' for him. His gut feel told him that the tender had been published with his company in mind. That part of 6.4 emphasising the *abroad* element was repeated in Schedule 4:

"The delegates must have an opportunity to visit and interact with some of the most successful local and global/international institutes and companies. There must be opportunities to explore the secrets of success from other developing and developed countries through engagement with successful leaders from leading institutions and companies. The programme must involve a visit to two countries; a developing country similar to South Africa that has advanced economically and socially, and a developed country."

They went into a lot of detail with Perseverance breaking down their strategy. One of the key elements that would make them stand out over other bidders, would be SAQA accreditation. They would communicate with their contacts abroad to find a reputable person with project management skills.

Overseas Again

To find someone with project management experience, and a solid track record in water and sanitation was not that difficult. A few names came up during pillow talk that very night. Felo had come across a few individuals through her work at the Council for Geo-Science. Fela concluded that it had to be a black woman in that role to score black economic empowerment points. She would be the co-ordinator of the entire project, taking delegates overseas when the time came. Patience would offer administration support services to the team, while Fela was going to be the 'chief of staff' for Waterwise Futurewise (Pty) Ltd.

The following week, on Monday morning Fela went to Pretoria for the tender briefing. The briefing hall was packed. The officials from the procurement department had not arrived yet, but the screen was up and the projector on. People seemed to know each other.

He overhead two of them gossiping about people who were walking in. 'Who wears an outfit like that," the one commented about a man wearing a cowboy hat, two-toned khaki shirt, denim shorts, long khaki socks pulled up just below his knees, and a pair of veld shoes. They made so much noise laughing, until someone shushed them.

The briefing was straightforward. It gave details about the process. At question time, Fela asked "Which criteria will you use to evaluate service providers?"

It was the first relevant question, which made the procurement officer take notice of Fela.

He put a new slide up, which read:

"Qualifying bidders must have at least 3 years' practical experience in conducting water related programmes with a solid footprint abroad,

- More than 8 yrs. – Excellent (8 points);
- +5 yrs. to 8 yrs. – Very Good (3 points)
- 3 yrs. to 5yrs – Good (1 point)"

He then explained that if an application did not make it through the first stage of evaluation, it would not be considered when they moved on to the pricing and fees stage. It didn't count if the bid was strong on price, but weak on methodology.

Then another hand went up. "Sorry sir. There is this concept that keeps coming up about overseas travel. Would it be permissible if I submitted a bid, with country names such as Nigeria or Namibia?" Everybody erupted into laughter. When they had calmed down, the procurement officer said:

"OVER SEAS means exactly that. You fly over the sea when you go to that country. Can you name one sea that you fly over when you go to Nigeria? None. Okay, so ladies and gentlemen, I want to emphasize this. We want our delegates to go and learn from economies that are doing better than us on water systems, not people who consult with us for infrastructure guidance and engineering expertise"

Fela, laughed all the way to the parking lot and all the way back to his home office. He was confident that the job was his. All details pointed in that direction.

When the office door swung open, Patience could not wait to ask him how the briefing had been.

"The scales are tilted in our favour. I'm glad I attended the briefing. I don't think I'd feel this confident if I had just filled in the forms and sent them by courier. There are a lot of chancers out there. Besides the laughable questions that some people asked, there was one guy in front of me with a tattoo sticking out over his collar. Can you believe it?"

Public-Private Partnerships

On the 10ᵗʰ of March, a month after they had submitted their application, an email came through from the department, congratulating them that they had made it through the evaluation stages, and were in the top three on the short list. They were invited to present to the procurement department and stakeholders from the Department.

That called for a celebration. Fela decided that if they managed to prepare all the source material for an impressive PowerPoint slide deck, by 14h00, they would take the rest of the afternoon off.

Patience then contacted their graphic designer, to ask him to put together a presentation for the following day. They only had until Friday to get everything together. In the four days, they also managed to get Felicia Gaylord to join their team. As it turned out, although she was a media analyst, she was also a seasoned project manager. Before the social entrepreneurship bug bit her, she had worked in a consultancy that provided water reticulation solutions to the mines municipalities.

Felo's contacts fell by the wayside. They demanded exorbitant compensation, making it clear that Fela needed them more than they needed him. Fela didn't have time for people who thought they were indispensable.

Fela and Felicia agreed that they would work on the presentation together. They would rehearse it over and over. They also prepared back up material in case there was a need for them to substantiate their claims. They had the two international institutions the delegates would visit on speed dial: the University for Peace in Costa Rica, and Western Washington University in Bellingham in the United States.

The presentation went very well. There were no glitches. Fela's stars had finally aligned. The only thing that was left was to pray for another few days while the final decision was being made.

On Tuesday afternoon, around 16h25 Fela received a call from the procurement officer from the tender briefing. "This is … errrrr the head of procurement from the Department of Water and Sanitation at head office in Pretoria. I am calling you Mr du Toit to congratulate you for winning the IEDP tender. Would you be available tomorrow morning at 10h00 for the official tender award ceremony at our offices?"

His heart beating heavily in his rib cage, he rolled down the windows of his bakkie, and said, "Yes sir. I know, uhmm I mean I will be available sir. I will drop everything sir. This is the best news I have heard in a long time. Thank you sir. See you tomorrow morning."

Even though the windows were open, he was gasping for air. He pulled over, and parked on the side of the road. He was so excited he wanted to sing the national anthem. He caused a lot of drama, with people driving past unable to resist the temptation of finding out what the crazy fellow was so excited about. Some even stopped their cars to hear him sing, *Nkosi Sikelel'iAfrika*. When he stopped singing he walked down to greet the crowds, and one small kid who was holding on to her mother's handbag, swinging it around, said, "Mommy why is this guy singing a funny tune of our play school songs?" and the mother shyly asked her which song she was referring to, and the child said, *"Incy wincy spider climbing down the wall"*.

11.   BENEATH THE ICEBERG

Children Witnessing a Parent's Arrest

The celebrations for the du Toits' clinching of the IEDP tender went on for the entire week, all the way to the weekend. Saturday morning started with Felo taking the kids out for a morning of fun and games at We Jump in Centurion. Each had to choose a friend from school, that they wanted to share that experience with. Felo's hands were full. Handling four children is not child's play. It would have helped if one of the mothers had come along with her.

When they got into her Tucson SUV she noticed that GJKK's friend buckled up, as soon as he got into his seat. She found that unusual for a boy his age. Buckling up in the backseat is not the first thing that pre-teens would do when they climb into a car. She was curious to find out what the story was with him. There is always a story behind people's behaviour. With children, it's even easier to find out, because the story might still be fresh in their minds. A question or two, could easily turn into a detailed rehash of an experience that they might have gone through recently.

"What's up with the belt honey? Are you good?" asked Felo while she looked at the kids from her rear view mirror, as she was driving out of the yard.

"I always buckle up Aunty Felo. I don't want trouble with the police like daddy on my birthday last year"

And right there, she knew she was right. There was a story behind that strange observance of the law. The boy's response was loaded. She carried on asking him questions, making sure not to open an emotional space the boy would find uncomfortable. She had to be gentle.

"What happened my boy? Do you mind telling the story?" she asked, with her voice and left hand gesture showing some sympathy.

"No I don't mind. We were coming back from a picnic at Zoo Lake with mommy and daddy. When we got home, we found a lot of cars outside our house. There were camera people all over, and a lot of police dogs and tough looking guys. They spoke with daddy. I didn't hear what they were saying. But I saw them putting handcuffs on him. They took him away. Then all of them went into our house, and turned it upside down. They took everything in daddy's study. And…. hmmmm….hnmmmm. Aaaaah…. heemmm. Sorry Aunty Felo, do you mind taking me back home now"

The boy sobbed heavily. The mood turned very sour in the car. She stopped the car. She then called his mother on her cell phone to find out if she was at home. She said she was there, but had a friend with her.

They drove there. At least it wasn't too far. It was only ten minutes away. They arrived at a palatial house in the leafy area of Midrand. Parked in the yard was a black AMG Mercedes Benz. Its windows were tainted. The number plate was personalised – *Zulu 6*. When the kids saw it, they were impressed and wanted to find out if it was his mother's other car. The boy said, "it must be mommy's friend, Uncle Z. That's what she said I must call him. He has a lot of cars, with the same number plate style. He's always here, since daddy left"

The kids jumped out of the car, to get a better look at the eye catching German machine, and to get a quick guided tour of the house if possible. The boy's mother was already waiting for them at the main entrance. She put on a brave face, and looked like she was hiding some deep emotional scars. She had bags under bloodshot eyes. Even her long eye-lashes, Brazilian weave and fancy Louis Vuitton top, could not disguise her pain.

She offered Felo a drink, who politely declined, saying she had to take the kids to We Jump as promised. The boy looked on, and Uncle Z emerged from behind the glass sliding door where he had been sitting on a recliner plastic chair facing the swimming pool.

He said hello to them, and disappeared down the passage. They said goodbye, and left.

Red Flags

That evening, Felo told Fela the story about GJKK's friend. She told him how emotional the boy got as he told the story of his father's arrest. The deep hurt he showed reliving the experience. They talked about it at great length. They didn't know much about the family, but Fela said he would find out.

On Monday morning, Fela shared the story with Patience and Perseverance. He shared the few details he had, and Perseverance said, "You don't know the guy? This story was in the papers for well over two years. The Hawks, Asset Forfeiture Unit and the Special Investigations Unit had been hunting him down for tender fraud and corruption in the Department of Water and Sanitation. It's only last year that they arrested him. They seized all sorts of classified documents they found at his house. I can still remember the headlines in one of the Sunday newspapers – *Nothi Boy Finally Behind Bars*, a story circulated far and wide, in boardrooms and bedrooms."

That really got Fela interested to find out more. Perseverance seemed to have a lot of details.

"I followed the story right from the day it went public. Let me tell you what happened. You see this Minister in the department now? She is new. She only took over in June, after a midnight cabinet reshuffle. The former minister was fired for her involvement in the scandal. When they fired her, she was redeployed to the Ministry of International Affairs. They then appointed her as an Ambassador to Chile, to go chill there, far away from public scrutiny. You see the problem with big tender contracts is that it gets everybody's eyes on you, as the winning tenderer. From government to fellow bidders who never made it, all the way to political parties who might have an interest in the work you have been appointed to do, or even crazy enough, you find yourself with relatives you never knew you had. That's why Fela, you need to stay far away from anything that smells like nepotism, graft, bribery, price-fixing, patronage, or collusion. This guy, Nothi, got caught up in an ugly web of greed and corruption, where he had to collude with other contractors who knew their bids were not as strong as his for the procurement of equipment that would be used by the department in fighting the sluice gate issues in all the 500 plus dams under the management of the department. It was a huge contract. In terms of technical competency, his bid was strong, but on pricing it was crazy. But they still appointed him. Prices had been inflated, to accommodate the demands of the cartel he worked with. He was a friend of the National Chairperson of SA Peoples Movement for Freedom, the ruling party. When all of this surfaced through the work of an investigative journalist, the Director General; the Deputy Director General and other officials implicated in that scandal were put on special leave pending the outcome of the official investigation and possible disciplinary processes. Some of the officials were arrested, but some are rumoured to be coming back from leave because no evidence of wrongdoing was found against them. Those who have strong political connections are most likely to be roaming the streets freely, very soon. You will see"

This really got Fela concerned. He was happy that he had brought a person with such exposure to what was going on in the country. He would not have had access to this information if he was working on his own. The extra eyes helped him see things he would have otherwise been blind to.

That was his first tender, and it was a big one. He had to go in with both eyes wide open. There was no time to be naïve. His reputation was very important to him. He would also never risk the safety and security of his family. His children were way too young to be exposed to any harsh realities in the country. He had worked very hard to get to where he was. There was a lot at stake.

Lucky enough for him, no one had approached him before the bidding process. He would have said no to it. But, judging by how skilful some of the fraudsters had become over the years, there were no guarantees. Confidence tricksters operate in mysterious ways. They are masters at the art of deceit, weaving webs of corruption.

It was important that they prepared themselves accordingly, so that nothing would catch them by surprise now that they had won the tender. Exercising foresight is rare, but it is necessary. While they deliberated, Patience was made notes on a flip chart:

- Questionable contract changes
- Suspicious documentation
- Dubious phone calls
- Irregular meeting requests
- Alterations on invoicing

Those were the main points they captured. Patience struggled to spell some of the big words, but Perseverance was always ready to correct her. He had been educated in Zimbabwe, where he grew up, during the old Cambridge Education system days. The roller coaster of life had brought him to South Africa in the late 90s when his county went through hyper-inflation. He married a South African woman, who was a domestic worker in Sandton. The two of them were thrown out of the back-room they lived in at his wife's employer when the madam of the house no longer wanted both husband and wife in the maid's quarters. Since then, they struggled to find decent, affordable accommodation. They moved from backyard to backyard, for years, until one day they stopped fighting. They accepted their circumstances and erected a corrugated iron shack in Alexandra. Because of his rare leadership skills and education, Perseverance quickly got noticed in his community and was appointed to serve in what was initially called the Alexandra Shack Dwellers Association.

Recalculating

Two weeks before the IEDP programme roll-out, Fela called together his project team for a full day session to recalculate and recalibrate for the highly demanding work they were about to do. They went through everything – administration; finance; legal;

compliance; logistics; travel; accommodation; venues; vehicles; communication; registers; time sheets; meetings; staff; training materials; assessments; evaluation; project stages; reporting; archives; itineraries; scheduling; media; publicity; tax; accounts; overseas expenses; exchange rates; visas; documentation; certification; food; entertainment; audits; insurance; medical cover; immunisation; evaluation and all other contingencies. They left no stone unturned. Felicia impressed them with her meticulous handling of fine details. Perseverance, as a former teacher, was also very helpful in advising on the delivery of the content, and working out how the course facilitators had to be trained on the pedagogy.

All the details from that day's outputs were integrated into the master plan, and reproduced in three formats, which they all got a copy of:

- 1 page concise Plan of Action
- 5 page Summary of Roles; Responsibilities and Scheduling
- 60 page Master Plan

On the wall, they posted a huge document, called The Four Agreements by Don Miguel Ruiz, which Fela wanted all of them to use as their personal guide throughout that process. He knew there were going to be highs and lows, and it was important that they could always rise above difficulties:

First Agreement: Be impeccable with your word

Speak with integrity. Say only what you mean. Avoid using the word to speak against yourself or to gossip about others. Use the power of your word in the direction of truth and love

Second Agreement: Don't take anything personally

Nothing others do is because of you. What others say and do is a projection of their

own reality, their own dream. When you are immune to the opinions and actions of

others, you won't be the victim of needless suffering.

Third Agreement: Don't make assumptions

Find the courage to ask questions and express what you really want. Communicate with others as clearly as you can to avoid misunderstandings, sadness, and drama. With just this one agreement, you can completely transform your life.

Fourth Agreement: Always do your best

Your best is going to change from moment to moment; it will be different when you are healthy as opposed to sick. Under any circumstance, simply do your best, and you will avoid self-judgement, self-abuse, and regret.

This set of agreements he had kept with him since he came back from Thailand; he only shared it with Felo. The awarding of the tender had a profound impact on how he approached his work and how he chose to work with his team. Their list of values for how they wanted to work were integrity, transparency and incorruptible honesty; followed by candid communication, with each other, the delegates and other stakeholders they were about to work with.

Fela spoke at length about the need for frank yet caring feedback. He wanted it to flow all the time. In his mind he knew that if they always showed how much they cared for each other and the work they were doing, giving each other feedback would not be a problem. He really wanted them to build deep, meaningful connections with each other.

One routine they agreed they were going to follow every morning before work was something they would call the Quotidian, a fancy French word that means routine. For Fela, rituals are important in building deep relationships in the workplace and at home. The Quotidian would be structured so that all of them took turns hosting it. There would be a facilitator every day, and participation would involve everyone. It would take only 30 minutes. They would do it religiously, whether they were facilitating on that day or they were just alone as a team.

The main points would be:

Gratitude: It was important that they would start the day by sharing what they were grateful for. It could be anything. It could be something that was happening at the time, or something that was about to happen, which they wanted to thank the universe for in advance, or something that the team had done or achieved together.

Reflections: Then they could reflect on what had happened the previous day; how they were feeling; what they did; and how things were going. An unreflected life is no life at all.

The 3A's:

Acknowledgement

Giving praise to each other in public was one practice that Fela wanted to instil in his team. The core team members, the facilitators and the support staff had to get into the rhythm of giving praise where it was due, and respect each other well enough to reprimand each other in private. Dignity and respect were a way of life that he wanted his team to be guided by.

Apologies

In order for them to recover from any petty squabbles amongst themselves or with the delegates, they also had to learn to be the first ones to apologize, before anything spilled over into a serious confrontation.

Ask

One other important aspect of this ritual, was to create an opportunity for the team to ask for help, assistance, favours from the team. Being able to open up about pressing needs, big or small would help them, cement the bonds they had with each other. If there was anything bothering them, they could address it right away. Nothing would pile up for long

Then there would be:

Inspiration: Anyone within the team could then share something inspirational with the team. It didn't matter if it was a poem, a song, an inspirational story or a funny cartoon they had cut out of a newspaper or magazine. The main objective was to start the day on a high note, fired up to take whatever the day was bringing with zest and gusto.

Intentions: Instead of talking about their to-do list for the day, they broadened it up by calling it a to-be list. The to-be list was an opportunity for them to share their intentions holistically. That covered a wide range of behaviours, attitudes and various approaches that would guide them as they did their work daily.

Braai Invitation

The joy that was felt in the du Toit household was contagious. It spread over to their neighbours, the Subramoneys. It even caught on with Thabo and his significant other, Dimples. On Thursday morning, Felo got a call just before she left for work. It was Thabang inviting them over to his town house in Centurion. He was hosting a braai, celebrating Dimples' 27th birthday. He told her there would be some of his colleagues from government and some old friends from his University of Pretoria days.

At the braai, that Saturday afternoon, they met all sorts of interesting characters. The men congregated more around the fire area in the garden outside, while the women were in the kitchen and lounge area. There was one guy whose interest was mainly about leading all new topics, and dominating the discussions, and be the one to see if it was time to move on to another topic. He was unusually tall and dark, but his scissor knees took away any thoughts of possible basketball involvement in his younger days. That is the reason why they called him *Kiss Madolo*, because of his knee formation. The ladies called him *Scissors*. He didn't mind. Some referred to his posh house in Centurion as Scissors Palace.

"But gents, what do you say about all this rampant corruption in newspapers almost daily now? What's happening with South Africa?" he said, with his squawky voice, while in his right hand he held a beer can.

"For me gents *neh*. The honeymoon is over for us. Mandela is going. The old guard of upstanding men and women who fought for our freedom in the trenches is now in their golden years. They are going gents. We are now left with vampires. People up there are just looting and looting. It's the politics of the stomach. They are lining up their pockets. Before we know it, we'll also turn into a banana republic. I am telling you" said the guy who had appointed himself the braai master for the day, so that he could be the one deciding which lamb chops would make it to the kitchen, and which would disappear at the braai stand.

That's when Kiss Madolo, took over and told them about an unfinished tender for an old age home. "Have you guys heard of a new phenomenon called proactive funding?"

"Proactive funding is when a minister is allowed to choose projects to fund before applications come in. This happened with the Dololo Old Age Home in the East Rand. It has been under construction for 25 months now, but there is only the foundation of the building to show for it. All this time it has laid dormant because of the investigations into what happened to the R30 million that was paid upfront for that project. One of my journo friends was there yesterday morning, for the site visit by officials, after a whistleblower brought this story to the attention of fraud watchers. Yooooh gents it's bad"

He took a sip of his beer, and carried on telling the story.

"They say according to the original agreement, the old age home was supposed to take six months to finish. A further R2 million a year was included to take care of running costs for the facility in its first three years." While Kiss Madolo was still enjoying the attention, one guy made a lousy comment to distract him and hopefully change the topic

"Anyway guys old age homes are not African. It's a foreign concept to us. Why would you want to get rid of your elders? They are the source of blessings. I don't support these European ideas, old age homes, children's homes, orphanages, psychiatric hospitals, horse peace and what what" he said, sounding intoxicated.

"It's called a hospice, by the way" said someone, before Kiss Madolo continued.

"As I was saying, the whole thing was messed up right from the word go. At registration stage, a bogus non-profit organisation certificate was used. When they traced the number, it actually belonged to another NPO in KZN province, which had nothing to do with the work. Apparently no one had bothered to verify the NPO number with the registry at the Department of Social Development. They also exaggerated the figures in their pricing and costs schedule. Here is how they got that right. They promised that the project would benefit a whole lot of people in the squatter camps in the area, but did not elaborate how that was going to happen. They said 100 children with disabilities were going to benefit from the facility. They claimed that 35 unemployed people would get jobs. But the funny thing is that the facility was designed in such a way that would accommodate 30 elderly citizens. In their justification, they called it indirect and direct beneficiation."

The guys were shocked. Fela never said a word, but was observing how such topics were handled by the guys. He paid particular attention to how none of them made any comments about anything that could be interpreted in a controversial way. That's exactly when the host himself said, "Gents you need to be careful of making career limiting comments. These are not just stories. They are about families and real lives. They are also about our principals in various departments. One slip of the tongue, you are gone *boetie*."

Unstacking the Deck

All those horrifying fraud and corruption stories were different cards in one deck. It needed careful consideration on Fela's part to be able to separate the cheese from the chalk. While he agreed that there was a need for exercising restraint, he didn't see how non-involvement was contributing to the urgently needed solutions. He felt that there had to be more people involved in the calling out corrupt practice. Looting of the country's coffers was going to get worse if people chose to play it safe. Even the jobs that they were so interested in preserving would be gone one day if the public purse had so many holes in it.

Corruption was slowly creeping into the public psyche of public. It tainted the image of black government officials. Sadly, very little was done to change it. Big money was siphoned out through agencies and other structures of government. It was at the centre of the social ills and strife seen in all spheres of society. Fela was in the system, but he did not want to be swallowed by the greed machine of the system.

Concentrated economic power begets concentrated political power. The corporations rigged the system in their favour. Waterwise Futurewise had to tread carefully when sourcing services or goods from big business for their tender, and also for other work they wanted to take on in the future.

It was great for Fela to learn all that within their first 18 months back in the country. Their hands were still clean, and their reputation was still intact. But, his trust in government had been sapped.

He took his work very seriously. Ethics was one area where he wanted to make a name for himself and his organization. His general outlook on life was different from the tenderpreneurs.

12.   FRACTURED MIRRORS

Water as a Mirror

You can tell a lot about a nation by looking at how it handles its water. All you have to do is to look at how the country's water resources are protected, managed, used, developed, conserved and controlled in a sustainable manner for the benefit of all its people and the environment. But then you can take an even closer look at how it manages its water knowledge systems, especially how well trained are the people entrusted with the design and effective implementation of policies, procedures, strategies and giving direction on how all of the water value chain aspects are handled.

That was how Waterwise Futurewise approached the IEDP process. They focused on transforming the whole person in the training programme and translating theory into practical application in the workplace. Their programme showed that they subscribed to the idea that "education is what education does".

In his international travels Fela had learned that fancy degrees are useless when theoretical knowledge is not converted into useful solutions on the ground. So they designed the IEDP accordingly: there would be pre-engagements with delegates before they met with them in person. This would help them preview delegate-readiness for the program. Pre-engagements would set the tone, to get them into a unique rhythm of training for development.

After the administrative aspects of the programme had been taken care of, they sent delegates links to two online assessments. The first was aimed at understanding the delegates at individual level. It looked at their preferred leadership qualities, behaviours, strengths and how they might possibly overplay them sometimes. Having that information provided insights into each candidate's persona levels, suppressions, derailers, enablers, key drivers, motivations, paradoxes, complexities and development needs. The second helped uncover how their teams perceived them; each candidate, they would be rated by seven coworkers – their manager; three colleagues at their level; and three direct reports. Feedback like this would help delegates see how they were received by others and how that impacted their work as managers and leaders.

The last aspect of the pre-engagements was a set of structured questions that each delegate had to answer and send back via email. The questions were:

1. What are the key challenges facing DWS at the moment?
2. What are the initiatives you believe DWS needs to focus on at operational level to resolve these challenges?
3. What do you believe might prevent you from achieving your goals as one of the leaders in the department?
4. How well positioned are you as a manager in meeting your department's goals and targets?
5. What value do you bring to your team and to DWS at large?
6. What are the main behaviours that you as a leader and a manager should demonstrate or role model to ensure successful strategy execution?
7. If you were to come out of the IEDP and say it was time well invested, what would have been the key critical outcomes from the program?

The delegates had a week to complete the three exercises and send them back to WF, for analysis. Going through all the input would require two full days of collaborative work between the two facilitators, Patience the administrator, Perseverance the logistics and liaison officer, Felicia the project co-ordinator, Fela the project leader.

When the contract was signed, and all details for the programme participants were finalised, they confirmed that there would be 20 candidates in total. There were two women, and eighteen men in the group. Six of the delegates were white; ten were black; three were 'coloured' and one was Indian. Fela was not excited about the gender mix. There wasn't anything he could do about it. They just had to make it work. They had to find a way of suppressing the high levels of testosterone in the room, when classes started.

The First Time Together

The programme participants came from all over the country. All of them were high ranking officials. Judging by the cars they drove, it was quite obvious that they had deep pockets. But judging by their attire, you would be forgiven if you thought they were farm owners. Those were men and women who spent their time in the offices and out in the sun, sweating it out in pumping stations and dams around the country. They came from different water boards; water user associations; the Water Research Commission; water trading entities; water tribunals and head office at the Department of Water & Sanitation in Pretoria.

To break the ice, when the first session started, Fela asked the same question that they had asked in the structured questions for pre-engagements.

"In order for you to come out of this programme feeling this was a great experience for you, it was time well spent and you would recommend it to others, how would you like the rest of the participants to treat you or deal with you?"

The first person whose hand shot up was a lady. She came across as poised, confident and clear about who she was and what she wanted to get out of the program.

"Hello everyone. My name is Nandi Sibiya. I am from the Umgeni Water Board in Durban. In order for this to work for me, there are few things I would appreciate from my fellow programme participants. As a woman, what I have to contend with whenever I am at work, or attending sessions like these, are mainly issues around being misunderstood and put in a box. I see it with my female colleagues at work, and I wouldn't want to see it happening here. When a woman asks hard questions during class, she is labelled as difficult. When a woman takes up space and is fully present in a session, she is thought of as being too much. When a woman is frank and tells the truth as it is, she is seen as troublesome. When a woman takes the lead, she is called bossy. I hope I am not being bossy already" She smiled warmly and sat down.

Her fellow delegates laughed, pretending that they were okay with everything she was saying. The facilitators could see that there was a lot for the men to chew on. To most of them, even though they wouldn't be brave enough to say it aloud, Nandi's words challenged their biases.

Fundamentally they did not see women as equally intelligent, deserving, and capable leaders.

All the candidates who spoke after Nandi were on a tightrope. They had to tip-toe a path through taboos, clichés and stereotypes, and hopefully make it onto solid ground. She had set the tone of the session. A tone that stamped authority, not just for her and the other lady in the room, but for all South African women in the workplace.

Her feminist introduction also put *her* in a tight spot. The men in the room, *did* think of her as difficult and troublesome. They didn't know any better. Most would blame it on their *culture*. Culture is a convenient scapegoat when misogynists can't formulate sound arguments. They will say things like, "in my culture women do not speak like that"; or even worse, "I can tell why there is no ring on that finger. No man can put up with this".

When individuals work together in a team for the first time, there is invariably some turbulence. As a facilitator you'd hopefully have the *super vision* to see the stage of development each programme participant is at.

Bruce Tuckman, in the mid-60s came up with a team development model called Forming-Storming-Norming-Performing. These phases are necessary for teams to grow together in a meaningful way. In any team, diverse or homogenous, it doesn't matter, there will always be challenges to deal with. Finding solutions, planning work and delivering results is not a straightforward process; teams don't automatically get together and deliver great results. Performance and productivity only follow once team members have settled on what is normal. Before that can happen, there may be some storms.

Nandi's words split the group in three. One group was obsessed with pleasing her. Another group sat on the fence: neither supportive of her views, nor necessarily having a problem with them. Then, there was the third group, the rabble rousers, narcissists and peddlers of stigma. One of them stood up, and said "My request is to her royal highness, Nandi Sibiya. I would like you to share the details of the book I saw sticking out of your handbag when we came in. I think I can learn a lot from it. It's called 'Men are from Earth, Women are from Earth, Deal with It?" As he sat down, eyes turned towards Nandi to see her reaction. Surprisingly, she was smiling warmly - unfazed by the provocation.

Then a Nandi fan bravely stood up, and told the previous person where to get off, concluding that he should apologize immediately.

"You see, that's what happens when you don't know your history. When I call her royalty, I am in fact complimenting her for having such an important name. The name of the mother of King Shaka, the great battle strategist and founder of the mighty Zulu nation. She was Shaka's closest confidant, one of the two most prominent feminists in Zulu history. The other being Mkabayi kaJama, Shaka's aunt. If it wasn't for Nandi, Shaka would have never made it to the throne. She fought for her son's rightful position in the young nation. Apologies if I sound like I'm giving you a lecture on Zulu history"

No one believed him. He didn't come across as sincere or of pure spirit. In his tone there was mockery. He was condescending.

One member of the Nandi group could not hold himself back: "I need to point out some things. Shaka's mother was *not* Nandi SIbiya. She was Nandi Mhlongo, the daughter of Bhebhe, chief of the eLangeni tribe, who were known as the people of the sun. The only Sibiya in Zulu royalty was Mthaniya. She was Shaka's grandmother, on his father's side. Through polygamous marriage practice, Mkabayi, singlehandedly courted Mthaniya for her father, Jama kaNdaba, who was aging without an heir from any of his wives to take over the throne when he was gone. She then agreed to marry the old king. She fell pregnant, and Senzangakhona was born. When finally there was an heir to the Zulu throne, the king was so pleased with Mthaniya, that he declared all the land on the South East coast of the Indian ocean, from south of the Komati River, all the way to the Drakensberg mountains, and the other side of the Tugela river, to be her land. In Zulu we say, *elika Mthaniya*, meaning all Zulu land belongs to Mthaniya."

When Fela noticed that people were misinterpreting Nandi, he intervened: "When you hear the statement that 'a woman without a man is like a fish without a bicycle', what thoughts come to mind?"

This provoked much reflection. There was a conversation about interdependence, not only between the genders, but across age groups, skill levels, experience, academic knowledge and so on. They ripped apart the notion that women's lives matter only when there is a man at the centre. This brought them to the question of leadership decisions in the workplace, specifically pay gaps between men and women, and the sharing of roles and responsibilities at work.

One man stood up and turned the conversation on its head, attacking lad culture. What about the pressure that men are under, where society at large, expects men to never show emotion? Male social inequality is also ignored. "Two months ago we buried my brother in the Free State. He committed suicide. It's socially acceptable for women to openly express their emotions. Why does this tolerance not extend to males as well? What I'm trying to say is, when we talk about what is the right thing to do for women, we should also talk about how we can solve the social issues around male discrimination and stereotypes too."

How the Medium Distorts Vision

It was important that they faced down the turbulent group dynamics. There was no way to avoid it, if they were sincere about forming a great team that could share powerful learning experiences and then perform well together. Pretending that feelings do not exist in groups, is a mistake. It sets the scene only for shallow engagement.

Then Fela and his team gave the delegates feedback about what their colleagues, direct reports and bosses back had said. Three things happen when you get an opportunity to hear what others think of you. Either you listen carefully to the words and phrases so that you can figure out *who* said it, so that you can safely ignore it; or you cherry pick the parts that boost your ego; or you feel compelled to justify, rationalise and defend yourself. Our natural inclination as humans is to seek cover. Fight or flight mode switches on, denying yourself the opportunity to convert feedback into a trajectory of personal development and growth in the organization.

"Let me start with a general overview. There are three points that we were measuring," said Fela as Perseverance put the individual reports on the table.

"The things we looked at were:

1. We wanted to get an understanding of what is going on in your head space, your individual concerns when giving direction and trying to lead responsibly. That involves how you, the leader, understands the business, sets direction, solves problems and makes decisions

2. Then we move to your heart space. This tells us about your concern for energy in your teams, how you think about enabling others and yourself. These leadership aspects are associated with the personal and the interpersonal, or your grasp of emotional intelligence.

3. From the head and the heart, we move finally to your hands. We want to know how you get things done. Not

done just for the sake of getting them out of your in tray, but done at an effective level, where you take pride in your work because you see it as your personal signature in the organization. This involves holding people accountable, ensuring that there are proper support and development processes in place for the people you lead, especially for those who need it most.

In summary, we looked at how the work of your hands, the energy beat in your heart and the stuff you think as you drive to work in the morning collectively impacts the people you work with. It tells a story about how others feel when you are around. How they receive you and how they experience you at work. "

That really caught their attention. Each and every one was alert now, and could not wait to hear the feedback. Felicia now read out a generic report for a fictitious character, focusing on the key points from each page of the report.

"I would like you all to understand that this is not about who is right and who is wrong. When you hear what others have to say about you, instead of saying 'I wonder who said that about me' or 'there is only person who speaks like that at work', I would encourage you to rather ask yourself this, 'What am I doing to create an impression so different to what I thought?"

She took them through the direct quotes, graphs, ratings and the analysis. She used a full hour before she opened the floor for questions. She asked them to not be shy, and to stop her if she was going too fast. The last thing she wanted was for them to feel they'd missed something. The department had spent a lot of money on the program, money that could not go to waste.

A person in the front put up his hand: "I see here on page 22, there is a question that says 'Describe what kind of behaviours he must stop doing in order to be an effective leader?' It says here I struggle with receiving constructive criticism aimed at improving my performance and the organization's results. It says I appear to be defensive and not open to suggestions. In a conflict situation I am condescending and dismissive, sometimes bordering on being disrespectful. I think those words are harsh, and not accurate. This comes straight from the mouth of someone I was competing with in the interviews for this post last year, and he never got the job. He is now out with his dagger to destroy me."

Felicia responded by asking "I would like to hear more of this story. How did others respond to the same question about you? How did you rate yourself on the very same questions? What are the things, in your view that you need to stop doing in order for you to thrive in your position?"

"I hear you. Well, there is this person, I can't really tell if it is a guy or not. This person says, 'He is not always consistent when it comes to applying policies, he is always trying to be accommodative and not always inclusive when it is needed'. While on my side I responded to that question by saying, 'I have to stop consulting too much and always seeking consensus amongst the team all the time. I trust too much. I always think that all my team members have the best interests of the organization at heart.' I think the second person's response was much closer to what I think of myself, but the first guy's comments were way out of tune."

Felicia could see that he was heading towards what in her coaching language is called, 'overextending towards seeking conflict and being argumentative'. This involves a pattern of behaviour in which someone likes to take charge and comes across as tough. Then when their toughness is challenged by someone else they escalate by being hyper argumentative and spoiling for a fight.

"I'm keen to understand why your colleague would rate you like that," Felicia replied calmly. "What do you think you do that makes people think of you in that way?"

He responded right away. His face was red, his tone of voice was stony. His posture suggested that he might soon throw a punch. "For me, as a manager at the coal face, at community level, on the ground, every day, what matters most to me is:

- Do people have access to clean water, that they can drink safely?

- How many households have access to piped water in their houses?
- How many households rely on communal taps?
- How many households fetch their water from rivers, streams, stagnant water pools, dams, wells and springs?
- What does that picture look like at national level, when you compare it with other provinces?
- What is the quality of the water? What do people say about it?

Where does water go? How is it consumed? What does the pie-chart look like?

If the answers to all these questions is a resounding *yes*, I'm happy. If other managers need their egos pampered, and their bums kissed, that's their problem. Period. Its not why I'm here. I want to get things done, not babysit or potty train anyone. If they have a problem with that, then when I go back to work next week after this block release, they will see whose ass is the blackest"

Reflection, Deflection and Refraction

At this point Fela realized it was time to weigh in. He'd given the speaker ample time to talk. Now he was just hijacking the class.

"Eish guys? What do you think is going on here?" Fela looked from one person to the next indicating that other voices needed to be heard, if any real learning was going to happen.

"In my view, this a classic case of how one single statement, can be blown up into a multitude of underlying single strands and threads. The danger, though, is the fact that most of what we're hearing is speculative, maybe even paranoid? It reminds me of high school physics. We would take a glass prism, and shine a light beam into it. Depending on the condition of the surface and the shape of the beam, that light ray would expand into a myriad of colours. It would then contract on the other side as a single light ray shooting out of them prism in a different direction. What we're dealing with is how the medium distorts the image. Depending on the angle at which you look at the light you can see two completely different things."

A few people clapped hands.

Fela went over to Nandi and gave her a high five. "Such words of wisdom. Spoken like a true scientist. I'm impressed that you steered the conversation away from the personal. Instead you focused on a core principles that is worthy of discussion," said Fela.

"In other words, Nandi, you are saying we are dealing with the conversations he is entertaining internally and he reads the comments from his colleagues and then internal starts expanding them to an even bigger version of what he thinks they are, while we as those listening to him, we see something else?" asked Fela

When Nandi confirmed that to be exactly what she was saying, Felicia then carried on. First, she tried to conclude on that matter before going back to the original section that she was on. She told them a story about what happens when people are not prepared to receive honest feedback from others.

"I am sure you all have met a long distance marathon runner. Well, I would like to tell you a story about an ultra-marathon runner. Let's just call him Sebastian. I like that name because I am trying to run away from what his farm workers called him, *baas*, and possibly what others in that little town of Villiers in the Free State called him, *Sir*. 'Sir Baas Tian' it is then. Okay? Sebastian was a leader who used a lot of red energy in his approach to almost everything. This meant that sometimes when he overextended, he drifted to the mode of being goal fixated, where he became rigid in his planning and would always stick to his plans no matter what. One day when he was preparing for participating in the Comrades Marathon, and on that particular year it was a down run from Pietermaritzburg to Durban, he sprained an ankle. He carried on training. The fact that he was injured did not stop him from sticking to his training schedule. He would strap a tight belt around his waist, so that he would attach a pouch for his painkillers that he would pop in every now and again to ease the pain as he ran. His wife would warn him about the possible dangers of not resting to take care of the wound. One day it just got worse. The ankle injury led to the snapping of the Achilles tendon on his right heel. That meant he could not run anymore. When others see what you can't see for yourself, and they tell you about it, it is important for you to interpret it as an act of love and kindness. When people stop giving you feedback, it could mean they actually do not care anymore. You are on your own. You don't want that. Be open to receiving constructive feedback. Use it, to transform to a better version of yourself"

Fourth Moment to Pause

1. When you are in a process of finding solutions, do you only aim for perfection?
2. How do you restrict yourself from being overly flexible and chaotic?
3. How do you restrict yourself from being so evidence-based that you get lost in the details?
4. When meeting people for the first time, what impressions do you tend to make?
5. What is your influence in group dynamics? What flavour do you add in teams?
6. What helps you to understand the context within which situations ferment?
7. What are the mirror distortions that could potentially cloud your vision?
8. How do you exercise restraint when you notice that you are overbearing?
9. When you find yourself no longer just accommodating, but acquiescing, what do you tend to do?
10. What are your triggers for passive behaviour and disengagement? How do you reconnect?

SECTION 5: BLINDSPOT (THE FUTURE)

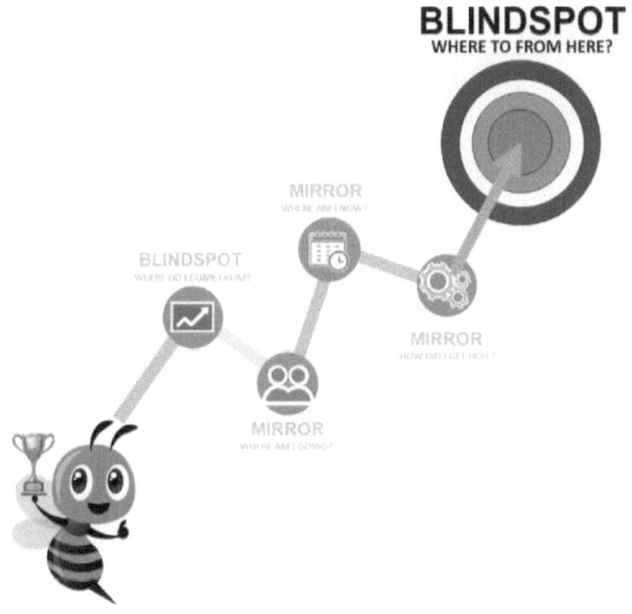

"Perhaps the best definition of progress would be the continuing efforts of men and women to narrow the gap between the convenience of the powers that be and the unwritten charter"

Nadine Gordimer

13. CONTESTED IDENTITIES

Appendages to Social Progress

The historical coordinates of the South Africa we live in today are not helpful in mapping out our future, despite our many uncoordinated, disappointingly chaotic efforts. If we are sincere about creating a truly inclusive society, new coordinates will have to be discovered. It is not like they don't exist. They do. We fail to see them because we have not made a commitment to digging deeper. You can't sketch out an accurate picture by leaving out the most useful details. We need to make a conscious effort to emancipate our collective hidden treasures, from our inexhaustible gold mines. They're within us. There are alternatives to supremacy, exclusion, deprivation, domination, elitism. The future need not be a direct extension of the past.

Borrowing from the words of Antonio Gramsci, our greatest threat is that while the old South Africa is slowly dying, the new is stubbornly refusing to take its rightful place under the African sun. It might be that our democracy was born bottom first. Ours was a breech birth. There is a lot we did not get right during our gestational phases pre-1994, during the build-up towards the new dispensation.

Felo would often ponder this conundrum. But she would seldom discuss it with her husband, Fela. Over the years she had matured. She was deeply aware of the cultural and political realities engulfing her and her new family. They affected her husband. He had gone through rapid stages of personal growth, self-awareness and social consciousness. The people who knew him from his early days as a learner official in Orkney could see it in him. They would tell him how surprised they were by how he manifested the promise of the rainbow nation. Many wished they could find their own new version, but so many barriers got in the way.

"Baby I hope you don't mind me saying this", said Felo, in a tone that announced itself as a prelude to a deep conversation. Fela knew what it looked like. She would sit on a chair with her right leg lifted up and kick off her sandals. She would twirl her index finger around her longest locks, and lean forward a bit. And Fela would know poetry, literature a mixed masala of thought experiments was in the offing.

"The conditions imposed on us by history have created more confusion, than solutions. Look at how difficult it is for white people to be led by black people. I have never been white, so I wouldn't know. Without sounding patronizing, I'm just trying to imagine what it must be like when you have to switch gears, from being a leader to being a follower. From what you tell me about the guys in your IEDP, for instance. Some of them don't know which mask to put on. In class they put on a mask that says, 'hey look at me, I'm tolerant' but back on the job, the mask they says, 'listen, I'm here to do the job I was appointed for. I am not here to be buddy-buddy with anyone'. Having a different face for a different audience must be a lot of admin. But then, on the other hand I also find myself thinking about the other side of the same coin. White people in South Africa have not really been victims of baneful oppression and exploitation. Yes, I know you will remind me of what happened during the South African War. The barbaric treatment of Afrikaans people by the English in concentration camps and so on. I am not talking about that. If you think of the …."

And then her phone rang. She rushed to get it.

The Duality of Inwardness and Outwardness

It was her brother Thabang, saying he was on his way over, with Dimples. She told Fela. He was always glad to see Thabang. They got along well. Having him around would give him a chance to share the final details about his imminent trip overseas with his DWS cohort. He expected Thabang to offer him some key points on what to look out for what to do with a group of senior government officials on a trip like that. Fela had heard the horror stories about how public officials booked on conferences overseas, would turn the whole trip into never-ending retail therapy.

"Hey *swaer*, how's it? Where are my little people? My two most favourite people on earth. How are the preps going? When are you guys going, by the way, said, Thabang as they gave each other the shoulder bump.

Felo came out to welcome them. And then Mali came over to give her uncle a hug, who picked her up and kissed her on the forehead. "I'm glad you're here uncle T. Daddy is leaving on Monday. Are you also going? Mommy said Daddy is going to spend lots of time overseas, and make lots and lots of money. So we won't see him much. Do you have a business, uncle T?" Everyone was dumbfounded. They all kept quiet. That's when Thabang reassured her, "no no my darling. It's not like that. Your dad is only going away for three weeks. He will speak to you over the phone, while he is overseas. And he will bring you nice things when he comes back."

Thabang and Dimples were there at Felo and Fela's place to let them know that they had decided to take their relationship to the next level. They were getting engaged soon. But, because the whole engagement process involved parallel processes, they wanted some guidance. On one hand there was the part about buying an expensive ring, and observing the Western cultural system. While on the other hand there was the part about sending a delegation of uncles to Dimples' home in Atteridgeville, for the pre-lobola negotiations. Both processes were looking like they were going to be expensive. Even more worrying for the two love birds, was the fact that the African part, could get very technical. Dimples' father was a staunch Zulu traditionalist, who had married a Pedi woman, when he started working as a bus driver in Pretoria in the mid-seventies. Even though he had spent all his adult life in the Pretoria West township of Atteridgeville, more than 600 km from his ancestral home in Zululand, he still remained an untamed Zulu warrior at heart.

To celebrate the good news, they decided to have a quick braai. Just the four of them, and the kids. No outsiders. The family bonds between them had just gone one notch up. Felo was relieved that her brother had done the right thing. In her heart, it always troubled her whenever she thought about her brother's real intentions.

Most of Thabang's age mates back in Burgersfort had children already, not just with women they were not married to, but with women they had no intentions whatsoever of marrying. In some cases, it would be two or three children per guy. All first borns. It was becoming a thing. Baby mama drama was the order of the day. In her mind, she simply could not fathom the idea of having to cover up or fill up the gap left by her baby brother if he ever fell for that trap and ended up being an absent father to multiple children out there. It frightened her.

"Ja swaer, we fly out Monday evening. Five to twelve midnight. We'll then be on an eleven hour twenty flight from Jo'burg to Amsterdam, flying KLM. At least the layover will only be an hour five. Then we fly out to Panama City, which is another eleven hours in the air. Then another two hours before connect to San Jose's Santa Maria International," said Fela.

"San Jose; Santa Maria, that sounds so Catholic. Saint Joseph and Saint Mary, Jerrrrr I feel for you guys. But aah well, I hear it's heavenly there. I am happy for you."

Thabang's dry sense of humour was so much more appealing to Fela, than the heavy stuff Felo was carrying on about before Thabang's call.

"But on a more serious note *swaer*. My little piece of advice to you and your team, as you prepare to take these public officials overseas, is that you must keep both of your eyes wide open. Nothing must miss you. As the person who is leading this learning experience for these people, you must be sensitive to the duality of what's going on inside of them and what you'll be able to see on the outside. These two realities are intertwined. A lot of what they will say in front of you compared to what they really feel inside is disjointed most of the time. That's the flux forced down their throats by their superiors. If you can't distinguish between the two, you'll miss a lot that can make or break the programme."

Learning To Listen, Learning To Talk

Monday came. All the delegates arrived on time at the airport, many accompanied by their families. They chose to all take up one area, and have a feast. It was their last supper together. Half of them had never been overseas before. The only thing international in their realities was Parys in the Free State, East London in the Eastern Cape, and Dundee in KZN. There was a lot of excitement in the air. The drama at the food court was palpable.

When all the church praise and worship songs had been sung, and the hugging ceremony was over, the IEDP delegation then meandered through the hallways, towards international departures upstairs on the east wing.

Check-in went surprisingly smoothly. Everyone was on their best behaviour. Until they got to the VIP lounge. One of the delegates had just come back from the liquor store, when he overheard a conversation between two Americans. Their distinctive accent was discernible by its twang and nasal sound. A black man was talking to a white woman. They were discussing their experiences during their stay in South Africa. They both seemed conversation perplexed by the race question in South Africa. The strange things they had observed and the funny stories they had heard.

Listening to them, talking about South Africa like that, was not an enjoyable experience. So he tapped Fela on the shoulder, and pointed his thumb towards the American duo.

"Are you hearing this?"

Fela listened for a while. Something compelled him to introduce himself. His accent confused them. They couldn't figure out if he was Australian or European. So they asked him where he was from.

"I am an African. I am a South African." That's what he told them.

They looked at each other, as if to say, "who between us is going to respond first?". "How can you call yourself African if you are white? Doesn't your whiteness disqualify you from that identity?" the woman asked.

"Being African is more than what my skin colour looks like. It's not about the coincidence of birth. It's also more than geography. It's a complex identity. If you want the two minute noodles answer, then you'll miss the nuances. When you are in Africa, Africa is born in you. Also, the skin colour dynamics you see here on the southern tip of the continent, are way different to what you'll encounter in the northern parts of our continent. Our brothers and sisters in Egypt, Libya, Tunisia, Morocco and other countries there are blessed with a different hue than mine, but still they are also African. Geographically they are closer to Europe than they are to the central parts of the continent. That doesn't make them less African than any of us here. When they speak they sound like the Arabs in the Middle East. The water between these land masses separates us. That's a topic I'm most interested in – how water separates nations."

14. DENYING MASCULINITY

Bearers of Polarized Character Types

What do you do when you find yourself on a long haul flight, and there are twenty two of you seated as a group? You engage in frivolous like getting into heated discussions about machismo and virility, hopefully without vulgarity.

"What you don't seem to understand is that you don't have to be male to have masculine traits," asserted Nandi, throwing a curveball into an already heated conversation. "You guys are approaching this topic from one direction only."

"Take for instance, executives like myself, who were baptized into boardroom politics by their male counterparts. When I started at Umgeni Water, in the mid-90s, there were no female managers. Not just that, but there were also no black people in managerial positions. The mentor assigned to me, was an Indian guy, who I really struggled to relate to. His idea of being in charge was that you had to be firm, economical with your words, keep to yourself, have barriers, principled and courageous. While I agree with some of those things, he came across as not accommodative to my femininity."

"So are you saying, there is a place for both femininity and masculinity in leadership?" asked the man next to her.

"For sure. I don't have to denounce my gender, and its glory, simply because I am in management now. I only learned this much later in my career. After a lot of trial and error. There's a lot of unlearning I had to do. For instance, in my first year as a manager I found myself in a robust confrontation, where we almost had blood on the walls of that tiny boardroom. We had a roadshow for water scarcity awareness week in the squatter camps around Durban and Pinetown. The GM spoke in a way that suggested my role was to do all the typically female stuff, because in his mind being female meant that I was naturally wired to handle soft issues and I had to stay away from anything that required physical strength or speaking in public, to address the crowds we were expecting. I was livid. I really had a go at his testosterone poisoned mind. I just couldn't handle men who peddled shallow gender assumptions."

A man sitting in front of her responded. "Back at home, in Parys, there is woman who killed her husband. Because the now popular gender based violence narrative has hijacked the psyche of social activists and the police, she pleaded innocence, claiming it was in self-defence. But after some serious digging by investigators, it turned out her husband had received a huge early retirement pay-out. He had started womanizing, and she wanted to put an end to all that. Her relatives told stories of how she wanted her husband to give her money to make extensions to their house in the township. The husband paid no attention to her. Instead he spent his money on loose women and girls. That's what pushed her to kill him. She went on to apply for a presidential pardon, on the grounds of femicide, but her application was turned down. That, in my view, is a classic case of how society polarizes the gender issues and takes advantage sometimes, to advance other agendas."

Bare Knuckles of the Bread Winner

That discussion went on and on, until it got the attention of Felicia. She brought a new twist to an already twisted discussion. "What do you guys feel about being married to a woman who earns more than you?"

"Yoh for me that's a big no no. My wife should never earn more than me. If she does, I don't think she would have any respect for me. The power scales would be tilted in her favour. Even the kids, would know, and not show much respect to me. Imagine my son growing up knowing that his mother was more powerful than me financially. Never!"

"I was once involved with a guy who earned less than me. It was a disaster" said Nandi. "He didn't know how to handle even simple things like who would pick up the bill when we were eating out. I noticed the discomfort once, at a hotel in Durban. We were sitting on the sundeck, on the rooftop. We ordered G & T", and just as she said that, one guy behind her tapped her on her shoulder asking what G & T was. And she told him it was gin and tonic. "We only had three rounds, and some pecan nuts, but when the bill came I saw him scratching his head. His forehead was furrowed, and his eyes were squinting. He studied each line in the bill. The waiter assumed that because he was the male, he was the one with the money. I was not really offended by that. But I must confess it was nice to watch him squirm a bit. Eventually he pulled his wallet slowly out of his pocket, and took out a bank card that I last used when I was a novice. He was embarrassed by the whole experience. In his eyes I could see him praying for the card not to be declined for insufficient funds. Luckily it didn't. Hahahhaaa. I would never marry a guy whose financial muscle is feeble and wiggly. Not because I place more value on money than love in relationships, but because of what men turn into when they are unable to provide."

Felicia pitched in. "What I find interesting is how a man's masculinity is measured according to how they are able to contribute to the family's economic situation. The interplay between the men and woman's role, as breadwinners and homemakers. I find it very fascinating. The privileges that men enjoy because of their financial contributions, and the entitlement that extends from there. When I was a child, there was this man in our street, who would beat up his wife if he came home from work and there was no food on the table. He had a good job at an insurance company. His wife was a home executive. At least that's what she called herself. Her biggest sin was that she was a gambler. Her husband would give her money at the end of the month, but hardly two weeks later, the cupboards would be empty. The casino was her second home. She gambled as if there was no tomorrow. Obviously, her husband would find out what she had done with the money, and his solution was to beat her up. Neighbours would hear her screams, and they would go to find out what was going on. When it really got ugly, the police would be called in. She was the punching bag for this guy."

The flight stewards enjoyed the camaraderie of the group. They kept the drinks coming, which kept the conversation flowing. Some would even stop to listen, or throw in a word to spice things up.

"My friends always say *oska bora moreki*, meaning, you must never upset the guy who pays the bills" one of the air hostesses said, as she pushed her trolley down the passage. When she walked away the conversation turned to the financial muscle in government. The *moreki* were their political principals, who had been appointed to senior positions as part of the cadre deployment policy of the ruling party. They talked about how much it frustrated them to know that they didn't really have power. All power was in the hands of the politicians. Most of whom didn't really have a good grasp of the technical aspects of the tasks they were overseeing. They were concerned about the sharp technical minds lost to the department because of suffocating, narrow minded policies. Most of those policies, were promulgated with the voter in mind, and not the water end user and consumer, as would have been expected.

It was these ambiguities that helped them to stay entertained throughout the first leg of their journey. They still had a long way to go.

Doing the Things Boys Do

The two layovers in Amsterdam and later in Panama City went by quickly enough. The only place there were issues was at Santa Maria International Airport in Costa Rica. A porter offered to push Nandi's trolley as she turned from the carousel towards customs. That immediately triggered some serious aggression on Nandi's part. She verbally attacked him. He didn't understand why she pounced on him. In his mind he was just being a gentleman; being helpful. Nandi didn't want anyone touching her bags, because of the drug stories she had heard about South America and the Caribbean islands.

Nandi had made her name in the group as the apprehensive activist. The men felt intimidated by her. Some tried hard to get her to confirm that they had no gender biases that. This only seemed to upset her. When they checked into the hotel, downtown, she was the first to choose the room she wanted to stay in. Everybody else had to wait. Even the man who had called her royalty, had no qualms about it.

They all checked in, eventually, and spent some time in their rooms before getting together in the dining area for lunch. They were starving, and had no time for speeches or long explanations of the itinerary. All they wanted was food. When it finally came, they were all quiet. Food in Costa Rica is second only to the country's natural beauty. It was a feast for the eyes and the stomach. They had *casado*, which was made with pork chops. *Casado* means marriage, because the dish is a coming together of many ingredients. There is rice, beans, salad, tortillas, fried platano maduro and meat. Just for good measure, there was also *chilero sauce*. They washed it down with fresh fruit juice.

After lunch they had the option of taking a nap (a siesta, as they call it in Spanish) or taking a stroll into town. Half decided to take the stroll. They wanted to explore the bars, and taste a bit of local beer. The one thing to avoid in bars was learning all the swear words, the first thing locals like to teach foreigners. Back in South Africa, an American expat once asked what the nicest thing was to say to a friendly boss, in Afrikaans. He was told "Just say *jou ma se hare*, they will love you to bits".

15. ON THE OTHER SIDE OF CAPITALISM

What the Scarcity Mindset Does

"I'm not really excited about the gilded furniture and all the grandeur around us, in this hotel or this country even. I don't mean to be a killjoy. But hey *boet*, face it. People back home in the Free State have serious water issues that need urgent attention from us. We are here getting pampered. The excuse is that we're being equipped to handle executive leadership demands. I'm not sure that sits so well with me. Look at the money that DWS has spent on this, and compare it to how many children could have proper toilets in schools back home. Think of the leaking pipes in most townships, how much money is the department losing there? Did we really have to come all the way here? And when you think about the next leg of this trip, how much more money will it cost the department for us to be at Western Washington University?"

The rant by one delegate, as they were sitting in the lobby, was strongly fermented by what they call in marketing 'buyer's remorse'. It borders on regret, distress, sorrow. He felt the department had to be penitent. There had to be a rethink on overseas travel costs, compared to opportunity costs.

"I agree with you" said a fellow delegate as he lit his cigarette and pulled the ash tray closer to him. "It's not like South Africa lacks funds or anything like that. We are a rich country. The problem, in my view, is how much our inferiority complex dwarfs our imaginations. When we want to train and develop executives, what do we do? We take them overseas. We even have the gall to emphasize that it has to be outside the African continent. Why? Because we don't think we as Africans are good enough. It's an insult."

"I don't care about fancy talk, fancy knowledge, fancy references. To me, it's just fluff. If you come to me and talk about economic theories, you must just know, you are not talking to me. And that's exactly what this trip is all about. And I am going to raise it. I want us to get real with each other. I want clear, practical action plans on how all of this translates into how a child benefits whose only opportunity for swimming is in the bilharzia prone streams of uThukela River tributaries in Vryheid, kwaCeza and Hluhluwe. I want us to come out of here with clear cut solutions, sustainable economic models that we can use in planning the household, natural and volunteer economy."

Their opportunity to vent was cut short by the receptionist who came over to them and politely said, *"Discuple, caballeros, no esta' permitido en el vestibule"*. One of them quickly pulled their one-size-fits-all one liner, *"Nosostros no hablamos Espanol"*. She responded with, "No hablo bien Ingles." When she pointed at the 'no smoking' sign, and made a hand gesture showed the smoking action, they knew they had to go outside. She didn't speak any English, and they didn't speak any Spanish, but the message was conveyed. They respected her, and walked out. On their way out, laughing, somebody said "so why have an ashtray on the coffee table, if smoking is not allowed?"

At the pool area outside, they found two ladies and a man, sitting around a metal garden table. They greeted them, and asked if they could join them. Luckily they spoke good English. They told them that they were from Sao Paulo in Brazil. And when they told them that they were from South Africa, their response was a unison expression of delight, "Aah Mandela," followed by "that was a great human being. Very inspirational. How are things in South Africa now that Mandela is gone?"

"Things are different now. The honeymoon is over. Now we're dealing with the real issues." This was met with curiosity. "Real issues like what?" to which the response was, "we were are talking about wasteful expenditure; about Africans learning to assert themselves; rethinking what our colonial masters shoved down our throats for over 300 hundred years."

This was something the Brazilians could relate to. The stories about squatter camps in Johannesburg; gangsters on the Cape Flats; corruption in all spheres of government; pit toilets in Eastern Cape schools. This was similar to the *favellas* on the outskirts of major cities. *Favellas* are shanty towns that start when squatters occupy vacant land at the edge of a city, and construct houses of 'salvaged' materials. The great wave of migration from the countryside to the cities in the 1940s to the 70s that was responsible for the proliferation of *favellas* in Brazil. Poor and confronted with the exorbitant costs of scarce urban land and housing, rural migrants had little choice but squatting.

"I don't understand why so many have to suffer indignity, poverty, when the world we live in has so much of everything. We have enough for all seven billon of us. What happened to us?" asked one of the Brazilians.

"I'll tell you what we've done. We adopted toxic ways. The way we play it, we put domination at the centre of everything. Man over man, man over woman, race over race, religion over religion, nation over nation. And the most costly one? Man over nature. We don't see ourselves as part of nature. In our arrogance, we raise ourselves above animals and plants. Think of how we speak as men. We say 'our women', 'our animals', 'our rivers'. Who said they are ours?"

A Rethink, Classroom Style

"Good morning everyone. I am Prof. Selbourne. I teach economics with a different flavour. You will pick it up in the title of today's lecture. I understand there are South Africans amongst us today. Welcome. I am sure you will find your stay here at the University for Peace, very fruitful and peaceful. All the stuff you'll learn in the classrooms and organizations you will be visit will benefit your country. I love South Africa. I was there for the World Cup.

The topic for today is a question: Because economic systems do not arise in a vacuum, what are they influenced by, and in turn how do they influence the larger cultural systems in which they are embedded?

Are you ready?

According to the PRB's World Population Data Sheet, an annual report that covers progress and challenges in 200 nations around the world, world population is expected to rise from 7.2 billion today to 9.7 billion by 2050. Virtually all this growth will be concentrated in the world's less developed countries, especially Africa.

So, how will population growth impact humans and the environment? Which prompts me to ask, how are we going to pursue sustainable economic development to meet human needs without sacrificing the environment?

While we celebrate all the great strides made over the past 50 years, we should not forget the huge price paid by the environment. Many indicators of the planet's health continue to decline. There's loss of biodiversity; carbon emissions and the big challenge of climate change. We need a rethink. A paradigm shift.

Asia is home to 60% of the world's population. China and India account for more than half of Asia's total population. By 2050, while birth rates decline steadily on a global basis, Africa's population will double, rising from 1.1 billion today to well over 2.2 billion. In Latin America and the Caribbean, people will continue leaving the region, mostly for North America and Europe. Immigration will be the highest driver of population growth in the US and Canada. In Europe, where birth rates have plummeted over the last few decades, the population is expected to decrease from 740 to 726 million by 2050. In Australia and New Zealand, the population will increase from 24 to 36 million and 4.3 to 5.5 million, respectively. This will be due to both immigration and a growth in birth rates.

What does all of this mean to you? What's your interpretation of what you are hearing here? As you reflect, what are your thoughts?"

Nandi's hand shot up, while others were still absorbing the predictions.

"You know Prof what you are saying makes me think how things have changed in South Africa. I don't know about the rest of the world, but let's assume similar trends. A simple change of habit – our sugar intake. We're shifting to honey, as an alternative source to sugar cane, grown in the southeastern part of our country. A documentary I was watching on the BBC, explained that bees are going extinct.

Bees are the biggest pollinators. They pollinate 70 of the 100 crops that feed 90% of the world. A world without bees, would struggle to sustain the lives of the billions of people. If you think of the fruits and vegetables we eat, and the animals that feed from crops, what would be their food source if the bees were gone?

The flower meadows where bees thrive are becoming a rare sight. The varroa mite that feasts on bee blood, climate change and the use of pesticides all pose a serious threat to the bee population"

A joker at the back of the class, making a cheap bid at popularity, said "Here I was thinking that fewer bees mean fewer bee stings." The class broke into laughter.

After a few more contributions from the class, the professor resumed his lecture, explaining how countries around the world were responding to the rise of China.

"China has asserted itself significantly over the last four decades, both culturally and economically. In 1978, when Deng Xiao-ping became chairman of the Chinese Communist Party, China's GDP was about $150 billion in constant US dollars. According to the World Bank, its economy has been recently growing to an alarming rate of $10 billion plus per annum. That's a constant annual growth rate of about 10%.

Those of us who are of a certain age, vividly remember the rise of Japan to world dominance in electronics, machine tools, semiconductors, steel and chemicals. Most developed economies at the time, were consumed by fear. That fear, impaired their vision.

How many observers could see beyond the rise of Japan and start being innovative.

What I want to know is, how your countries are responding to the rise of China? How have Chinese goods, and Chinese culture infiltrated economic spaces in the countries you come from?"

An African man, with a slight American accent spoke up. "The rise of China has really messed things up in East Africa. Our governments took on big infrastructure development loans from China. Now they're struggling to pay them back, so China with its stronger financial muscles, owns and controls assets that should belong to Africans. It's like a second wave of colonization'. In hotels these days it's quite common to find two food serving counters, one for locals and another for the Chinese palate. In some schools, kids now have the option to study Mandarin. Chinese imports are of low quality, but they're cheap. It has destroyed our manufacturing capacity in textiles and clothing. Also, several big retailers who can't compete with Chinese pricing have closed down."

A woman sitting next to him, who introduced herself as South African but not from the DWS group, said "I'd like to bring another dimension to this topic. We need to include questions around the real wealth of nations, which is its people and its natural endowments. Take South Africa for instance, after the Mandela years. Look at the decay, and the eating away of the human spirit and soul. We are well endowed with gold, platinum, chrome, coal, and many other minerals. Coal from our mines in Zululand is of very high calorific value, with low ash content. Zululand anthracite has a caloric value of well over 25 MJ/kg. This is exported to rich industrial nations all over the world, yet when you go to where those mines are, you will be greeted by abject poverty in the villages where I grew up, kwaNgwabi, eMpakama and oKhukho. It's an injustice, and a gross violation of human dignity on many levels."

When she got emotional, the professor suggested a short break.

Beyond the Banks of the Orange and Vaal Rivers

The lecture carried on, but Fela and Felicia, didn't attend after break. Instead they went to the restaurant to do a bit of administrative work. The first thing was to report back to the Department of Water and Sanitation, back home, on the first half of Day 1 of lectures, and explain what was expected to happen for the rest of the week.

With the formalities taken care of, Fela then called Felo in Midrand. He struggled at first to confirm the time difference, and what Felo and the kids were doing. He waited until he was sure it was almost dinner time, and all three were sure to be home.

"…I really miss you guys. I so wish you were here as well. We are learning so much. All of a sudden everybody has lightened up. They're very receptive to what they're learning. The bonds have grown stronger. The influence of the delegates from other parts of the world is amazing. You can see how they are cross-pollinating from each other's knowledge, experiences, and attitudes. I'm glad we did this. I can't wait to be back home to take this work to another level. Touching lives. Making a meaningful contribution. Developing more leaders. I will forever be grateful for this experience and the memories we're creating. But hey, what can I say, I also have limitations. I am just human, *ke Motho Fela*."

Fifth Moment to Pause

1. When considering the challenges nationally, where is all the exceptionalism coming from?
2. How are you confronting global issues, especially how they impact on you personally?
3. How do you contribute towards the creation of high performing teams, especially in a crisis?
4. Do you hold your leaders accountable, while maintaining cordial relations?
5. When you are under pressure, how do your strengths become unconstructive?
6. In group dynamics and conversations, what energies do you normally get drawn towards?
7. How do you think people would respond if you started showing up unmasked?
8. What is about who you true are, that you need to return to?
9. As you march towards an unknown future, how are you improving your visual acuity?
10. When you achieve what you've always wanted, what will you be aiming at, next?